ABOUT THE AUTHORS . . .

Maria Augusta Trapp grew up in Austria and became the second wife of Baron Georg von Trapp and second mother to his seven children. The story of how Maria became governess for the children upon the death of the first Baroness von Trapp, and her eventual marriage to the Baron has already been told in her first book, *The Story of the Trapp Family Singers*—from which the phenomenally successful musical, *The Sound of Music*, was adapted.

The second marriage was blessed with three more children making a total of twelve golden voices in all. Soon after their arrival in America, the Trapp family—with Mrs. Trapp as a guiding force—began a highly successful career as professional musicians. But Maria Trapp is not only a mother, musician, homemaker, and world traveler, she is also an accomplished writer. *The Story of the Trapp Family Singers* won the Catholic Writers Guild annual St. Francis de Sales Golden Book Award for the best book of non-fiction in 1950. A *Family on Wheels* is an equally delightful story.

Ruth T. Murdoch, who has been a close friend of Maria Trapp for many years, holds B.A. and M.A. degrees from Vassar College and a Ph.D. degree from Columbia University. She has taught French at Smith College and is now Assistant Dean and Associate Professor of French at Manhattanville College of the Sacred Heart.

The Story of the Trapp Family Singers is also available in Image Books – Image D 6.

A FAMILY ON WHEELS

Further Adventures of the

TRAPP FAMILY SINGERS

BY

MARIA AUGUSTA TRAPP

WITH

RUTH T. MURDOCH

CONTENTS

1

González

How clearly little things can bring home to our hearts the truth we are trying not to know. González broke. He broke the day before Christmas, 1955, just after we had reached home; and I finally understood that the Trapp Family Singers had completed their farewell tour.

González was a small mechanical monkey. To explain his name is a story in itself. It is enough to say here that he had a sad-funny face, a red bonnet, and cymbals on his paws. Through the long, last tour he had been our helpful friend and mascot. Each time we wound him up, we were sure of his enthusiastic applause, and he kept us humble by stopping short in exactly ten seconds. Now it was all over—and González was broken.

We had come together after lunch for a few quick minutes in the big bay window of our Vermont home, Cor Unum —quick minutes, since, no matter how tiring the last concerts had been, everyone's mind was racing with mysterious Christmas plans to be completed within the next few hours. Outside a cold straight rain—*Schnurlregen*, we used to say in Salzburg—hid the Worcester Range and the hills of Stowe that remind us so much of Austria. Inside, the house smelled of Christmas greens. A great wood fire crackled in the fireplace, shone brightly on the fir Advent wreath hanging from the ceiling, and made shadows on the mantel across the carved wood figures of Our Lord and His twelve Apostles. In the bay window, Agathe was pouring coffee from the round

copper pot, Maria was helping her to pass the familiar blue
cups, and Monsignor Wasner, our conductor, was hoping out
loud that he had not been given too much cream. Lorli
(whose name, when we remember it, is Eleonore) was knitting, against time, on a Christmas present, and Johannes had
been sent for more wood. (At seventeen Johannes was always
being sent for more wood.)

Suddenly González, who had been given a dignified place
of honor in the middle of the coffee table, coughed a deep
mechanical cough, clapped once, and froze. Just who had
wound him up? I do not remember, but each reaction was
typical. Rosmarie shook González once, and Monsignor Wasner shook him three times. "Try him on a little coffee," said
Werner. Werner and Erika had five children. Their household, just down the road from Cor Unum, was not unused
to such happenings. Agathe quietly went on pouring. Maria
laughed. Maria's laugh is her specialty—Johannes once suggested that it should be recorded and the record sold in hospitals.

"He looks," Maria said, "as though he'd been asked to learn
a new song on ten minutes' notice!"

Monsignor Wasner did not understand why everyone
thought this funny.

"Maybe Elizabeth can fix him," Lorli suggested.

Elizabeth, aged nine months, was just like my little Lorli
as a baby—all round cheeks and black eyes and mischief. She
had left Mother Lorli's lap to slide down behind the chair
of her father, Hugh Campbell, and turned out to be busily
"fixing"—by tearing it to bits—our latest copy of *The Burlington Free Press*.

Meanwhile, Hedwig was full of extroverted ideas about
first aid for González. Hedwig is always bursting with ideas.
You can hear her thinking out loud (in top soprano tones)
all over the house, although professionally she is a first alto.
The trouble is, she is usually right, but now even her best
efforts did not help. By the time she had everything *inside*
González *outside* González, we all had to admit that his ill-

ness was deep-seated and permanent. Rosmarie reassembled him for the sake of appearances.

For a few minutes, after the others had scattered, I remained behind in the bay window. González was looking at me with his paws up in an air of permanent surprise.

"Poor little monkey," I said. "Maria is wrong. The trouble is, there *is* no new song to learn."

We had certainly never expected to go on singing forever. In fact, we were constantly being surprised that year after year people in Florida and California and New York still seemed to want us. By ourselves, we had never really planned to sing at all. Our home was Salzburg, where Baron Georg von Trapp, "Der Trapp," a naval war hero, had married me after the loss of his first wife—but this is a twice-told tale from *The Story of the Trapp Family Singers*. I need only say that, as a singing family, we had fled from Hitler in 1939: the "Captain" and I; our priest-friend, Father Wasner; the older children—Rupert, Agathe, Werner, Maria, Hedwig, Johanna, Martina; plus our more recent additions, my own Rosmarie and Lorli. Little Johannes was also with us at the time although, as Lorli said, "You didn't see him yet."

As a singing family we had played, prayed and stayed together through hardships and joys in the long years of our American homemaking. Then there were weddings: Rupert and Henriette; Johanna and Ernst; Werner and Erika; Martina and Jean; Lorli and Hugh. Our first deep sorrow came in 1947 with the death of the Captain, our father, my husband—then four years later, the sudden loss of Martina in childbirth.

So many changes had meant choral changes as well, and from time to time new members for our singing family; but, all in all, for nearly twenty years we had sung our way across Europe, North America, South America, Hawaii, New Zealand, and Australia—and it was really time to stop. Rosmarie, advised by a doctor to stop her concert activity, no longer sang with us. Lorli, our top soprano, had left us two years ago. Now Werner had been asked to help in the work of founding a music school. Besides, he really preferred his own wife and children to the children of Europe, North America, South

America, Hawaii, and so forth. So, with joy and sorrow, we had sung our last concert. Once more, in the adventure of faith, a door was closing, and I could not believe it. So González was sitting among the empty coffee cups explaining it to me, while I explained it to him.

The rain was turning to snow. Through the bay window I could see Werner and Hugh heading out towards our little cemetery with green wreaths for the Captain and Martina. Werner was carrying the Captain's ship's lantern, which I knew had been just freshly trimmed and filled for Christmas Eve.

"Dear Georg," I said softly, watching them make their way across the field. "What comes next? We are all pretending that things are just the same, and each one knows that this may be our last Christmas together at Cor Unum. Help us make it one of the best ever—"

It *was* one of the best ever. By late afternoon the giant Christmas tree was groaning with candy and cookies, and glowing with wax candles. In the great living room of the guest wing, behind closed doors (for everyone knows that the Christ Child Himself arranges these things), a huge ping-pong table had been heaped—nearly to the ceiling—with mysterious packages: "To Agathe from her Kristkindl," "Mother from ——," "Father Wasner from ——," "For Hedwig with love, ——." The kitchen smelled of fresh bread, Pfeffernüsse, and Lebkuchen; and in a corner the Christmas goose, which had just been taken from the freezer, sat obediently unfreezing, propped up and looking, as Hugh said, "as though it had tried too hard to learn an Austrian folk dance."

At five o'clock everyone gathered in the chapel where Maria and Erika had hung garlands of ground pine around the old Spanish crucifix and lit wax candles on the fresh Christmas trees either side of the altar. Only a few "non-Trapps" had come to be with us—Louella Apiki, the "adopted" Hawaiian member of our family; Rosemary Glynn, my secretary; several ski guests; one or two close friends. Werner and Erika had brought their family, all dressed in Sunday best, and little Elizabeth proudly wore her first Austrian dirndl, a creation exactly thirteen inches long.

Together we prayed the Rosary; and, in the silence following the last "Amen," came the faint ringing of a silver bell calling us all over to the guest wing. Someone had trimmed the long corridor with a gay line of paper Christmas trees, and Rosmarie had put a gingerbread man in each window.

At the far end of the great "guest" living room, a fresh fire burned warmly. In the soft light of the Christmas candles, we quietly formed a circle. When we were all present and everyone was still, little Barbara, Werner's oldest daughter, stepped forward and recited the Christmas story. (Before Johannes was born, we had planned to call him Barbara— and how surprised we were when all his baby-clothes had to be hastily remade! Now, our real Barbara was at last old enough to take his place at this important moment on Christmas Eve.)

As Barbara finished, looking up at her mother for approval, we began our favorite *Stille Nacht*—in English, so that every guest could join in.

" 'Sleep in heavenly peace' "—when the last notes had died away, and with Elizabeth already wriggling towards the presents, we wished one another "A blessed Christmas." Finally, through oh's and ah's and a rising tide of Christmas wrappings, we retired for a few hours' sleep. I think Johannes took his new rifle to bed with him.

Just after eleven came Monsignor Wasner's voice sounding through the darkened house:

> *"Hirten auf um Mitternacht,*
> *Erhebt euch aus dem Schlafe."*
> ("Shepherds, up, your watch to take!
> Your time of sleep is ending!")

It is only too true that, with the best intentions in the world, some of our "shepherds" wake less quickly than others, but on this particular Christmas Eve, they outdid themselves. Dear Father Wasner! The result was that, for the first time

in twenty years, we heard him sing the old traditional carol
in a new version, spontaneous and unrehearsed:

"Hi-irten auf um Mitternacht—"

Pause. Silence.

"Hi-irten auf um Mitternacht—"

Pause.

*"Hi-irten auf um Mitter—*SAY, COME ON!*—nacht."*

The effect was immediate. Laughing, struggling into caps and
jackets, we all gathered quickly in the hall, each one joining
in the song. Jeep trucks took us down the hill through the
deepening snow to the little village church in Stowe, where
we sang a Solemn High Mass, and by half-past one we were
back in the chapel at Cor Unum for three Christmas Masses
of our own. We sang our favorite songs—*Quem Pastores
Laudavere, Es ist ein Rose entsprungen, The Virgin's Lullaby;*
and outside, across the fields, the clear beam of a lighted ship's
lantern came to us through the falling snow.

Then everyone gathered once more in the Cor Unum living room. It was too late to go to bed, and too early to get up.
From the kitchen Agathe and Marie produced hot Würstl,
cookies and a steaming Christmas punch. Johannes was sent
(of course) for more wood. Just how long we sat talking
around the fire, I do not remember. One of our priest-visitors
was circulating a pencil and paper from one person to another. In a few days he would be leaving for Rome and had
promised each of us to offer Holy Mass at any spot on his
itinerary we might choose. Maria wanted Lourdes, and I
begged for the Chapel of Mater Admirabilis in the Sacred
Heart Convent in Rome.

When at last the list was complete, someone asked casually, "Where will you be one month from today, Father?"

Our guest took the question seriously and was silent for a
moment. I can still see his lean figure bending over to knock
his pipe against a stone of the fireplace.

"Where I will be is not very important," he answered

slowly, straightening up, "but tell me how I must think of *you*. Just what will you all be doing?"

Suddenly the secret question was stretched out in front of us as bare and exposed as the last Christmas cookie on an empty plate. Monsignor Wasner was the first to answer: "Expecting a letter from my Archbishop." Would he now be recalled to Austria?

"Heading back to Hawaii," said Louella uncertainly.

"Looking for a house in Pennsylvania," murmured Werner. No one else spoke.

"Mother," and Rosmarie turned to me, "what will you do next?"

For a long moment I watched the rosy glow of the fire and the little figures on the mantel. Somewhere in the back of my mind, I could hear the voice of the Apostolic Delegate in Sydney, Australia, saying: "If the Trapp Family ever stops singing, let me know—" but his words sounded very far away.

"I think," I found myself saying, "that before I decide, there should be another book written."

"What about?" Johannes liked facts.

"A book," I answered, "about all the things that have happened on our tours as a singing family."

"Good," said Hedwig briskly, "and while you are writing it, I will clean out the barn. That will take care of me until 1960 at least!"

A general laugh cleared the air, and everyone was suddenly full of suggestions for me:

"Mother, you could begin with how it was in the bus—"

"Remember New Zealand and the Maori dances?"

"And the time the pilot turned the plane around in South America—"

"Tell how Johannes fell asleep on the stage in Cuba—"

Mother this, Mother, this. This in Miami, this in Calgary, in Munich, in Buenos Aires, in New Orleans, in Honolulu—

Finally, Louella asked us to sing the beautiful Hawaiian song of parting, *Aloha Oe*. One of the guests wanted *The Virgin's Lullaby* again. We drifted to *Stille Nacht* and on into a Swedish carol. Then, suddenly, we were singing, singing, singing, everything we knew—Austrian songs, German songs,

French songs; songs from New Zealand, Australia, Brazil, Puerto Rico, Hawaii—while Monsignor Wasner's eloquent hands drew us from one cadence to another as we sang with one voice until we were spent with singing, and Johannes' fire slowly and inevitably burned down, glowed red, went out—

It was nearly dawn on this Christmas morning of 1955 when I finally reached my own room, my head buzzing with songs, sleepiness and ideas for the story of our "life on wheels." The cold night had put a heavy lace curtain of frost on each window, and a fire had been kept going on the hearth. I crossed the room, struggled for a moment with a frozen catch, then swung open the window, and a great gust of cold mountain air came rushing in. Outside, the snow had stopped, the sky was a deep gray-blue, and the dark hills and trees were silent in a cold hush of quiet waiting. As I stood there, breathing deeply, my husband's voice came to me: "Whenever God closes a door, He opens a window."

He had said that in 1939, in our days of painful uncertainty. Suddenly I was deeply ashamed. Through a great fringe of icicles hanging along the eaves, I could see Georg's ship's lantern, still burning steadily; and, next to it, on Martina's grave, a cluster of colored Christmas lights seemed to cling like a gay little brooch. In that moment my question marks for the future began to disappear. How stupid! We had all been so busy closing the door that no one had looked for a window. We had turned back to the old songs because we could not quite bear the thought of a new one. We had completely missed the words of the Third Mass for Christmas Day; "Sing joyfully to God—for this day a great light hath descended upon the earth." . . . "Sing ye to the Lord a new canticle, for He hath done wonderful things."

I began to see that each one of us must wait in faith to find the new canticle. Little did I know then how soon and to what strange lands it might take us—first Rosmarie, Maria, Johannes; then, later, Monsignor Wasner and myself.

If I could have foreseen—but I could not foresee. Tomorrow I would begin work on the new book. Already my mind was going back to the tours of other years.

2

A *Family* on *Wheels*

It was a Tuesday morning in September—I think the exact year was 1949—a crisp sunny morning for the start of our fall tour, with the mountains around us flaming scarlet and gold, and the Stowe Valley blanketed in a heavy white mist.

"Nine o'clock rolling!" said Father Wasner.

"Nine o'clock r-r-rolling!" Johannes' boy soprano picked up the words and sang them out with all the force of his ten-year-old lung power. In the long pine-paneled dining room at Cor Unum cups clattered quickly into saucers as everyone arose from the table. We knew our signal.

Outside, the big blue bus of the Cosmopolitan Tourist Company waited under the poplar tree, while Dave, the driver, prepared to deal with our luggage. We had just half an hour to check on all final details—half an hour, and well we knew that "rolling," for Father Wasner, meant a bus nearly out of the driveway with everyone seated and the driver already shifting into third gear. We scattered.

Last-minute luggage was still an agony, even though we had learned a great deal since the early days when fifty-four separate items accompanied each departure. Now, in the morning sunlight Dave and the boys stowed concert equipment first of all: three large suitcases with the costumes; Werner's viola da gamba; the spinet in its case, with—last and very precious—a blue cloth bag containing its detachable legs. This little item had its own malicious way of staying behind.

Next, Father Wasner brought out boxes of music, books,

and his priestly vestments. Martina put in her paints, and
Agathe turned up with a small sewing-machine. Maria saw
to it that the ten recorders and her accordion were given a
seat to themselves. Johannes did likewise for his nature collection and a battered coonskin cap. In addition, each girl
packed one medium suitcase and her "mops," an overstuffed
hand satchel that looked for all the world like a fat little lap-
dog.

As for Mother—my needs had long since been reduced to a
modest minimum which I had carefully assembled in my
room, and which Werner, Dave, Johannes, and two farm
boys now managed, staggering, to carry downstairs for me.
First came my "mops" and suitcase, a large carton of books
and a guitar; then a dictaphone in two parts (referred to as
"Peter" and "Paul"); a typewriter, and a briefcase of correspondence. These were followed by an old-fashioned mechanical blender, nicknamed the "DC-3" because of its incredible grinding noises while converting carrots, spinach,
parsley, peppers, celery or tomatoes into the liquid vitamins
and minerals indispensable to any trip. Next, understandably
enough, came quite a few large paper bags filled with carrots,
spinach, parsley, peppers, celery, and tomatoes. Last of all,
there was my heart's treasure, the Dormiphone—a fine instrument designed to teach languages by gently playing language records through one's sleep. A clock turns it on, an
earphone under the pillow does the rest—and, in no time at
all, one wakes up talking French fluently.

(During that whole tour, I might add, I never once awoke
talking French fluently, though I occasionally got out of bed
muttering, "Le grand-père est assis dans sa chaise. La grand'-
mère est assise devant la table. Le père et la mère sont assis
sur le canapé. Les enfants sont assis par terre." Finally, sick
and tired of helping that family sit around, I bought a few
records, set the alarm, and woke up to the music of Bruckner's
Fourth Symphony.)

At last all was ready. Then came tearful farewells: to Jean,
Martina's husband, who would join us after a few weeks; to
Pierre and Thérèse, to Julie Cannan and Tante Caro, the

"old faithfuls" who would take care of the farm in our absence; to Erika, whose little Barbara was to arrive in a few
months. Then heads were quickly counted as everyone
climbed aboard. Dave blew loudly on the horn, the door of
the bus slammed, and the wheels began to roll.

Father Wasner looked at his watch. "Ten minutes late,"
he said reproachfully.

As the great vehicle moved slowly down the mountainside,
I checked anxiously once again. Had no one been left this
time by mistake? Johannes, who loved to "pilot," was standing in front, close to Dave. Behind him, in the first seat, sat
Agathe, our oldest daughter; and across the aisle from her
Hester Root, my secretary in those earlier years, was already
busily arranging an "office" with stationery, carbon paper,
typewriter, and paper clips.

"Dave, please stop in Stowe so I can phone Jean. I forgot
something." Yes, Martina was definitely aboard.

In the rear of the bus, where several seats had been removed, Werner had arranged his belongings, which included
a hand loom. A comfortable cot bed had also been set up,
for anyone who might wish to rest during the long ride.

I could see Maria sitting relaxedly among her recorders,
with the accordion on the seat next to hers; while Hedwig,
after much puffing and pushing, had arranged herself beside a
pile of heavy boxes containing leather work and tools. Directly behind me, Illi (our nickname for Rosmarie) and Lorli
were chatting animatedly. I hope, I thought to myself, that
Lorli won't have those headaches this year. She was subject
to severe carsickness at times.

The center of the bus had been converted into a "living
room" by turning two seats on each side to face the others.
My place was always there, on the right—and on the left,
though I still could not believe it, my husband's place was
vacant. Now, as I looked over, I saw that Father Wasner had
thoughtfully taken a seat there to fill the sad emptiness. Yes,
all were present and accounted for.

In Stowe Village we made two emergency stops: one for

the mail, one for Martina's call to her husband; then the wheels turned south.

"Dave," Johannes asked, "which route do we take this time?"

"Number 7 from Burlington, leading into 22. Destination—New York City!"

New York, for business reasons, was frequently our first stop, no matter which direction we might be going afterwards. For this particular tour, I knew that our first concert would be in Caribou, Maine. Beyond that, I had not yet checked the itinerary. If it were like that of previous years, we would probably go west into Canada, then out to Chicago and back to Kentucky. In early December we might come north through Virginia and Pennsylvania to Buffalo and east to Boston—until finally, just before Christmas, we would be back in New York again for the Town Hall concerts.

Years before, during our earliest tours, we had been indignant about the routing and full of such suggestions as:

"Why must we go first to Bryn Mawr and then back to New Brunswick?"

"Wouldn't it have been much more practical to put Fredericksburg first, instead of having us go down to Bristol and then return? We could have saved three hundred and forty-eight miles!"

Or:

"Look—this makes us detour three hundred miles, one hundred and fifty miles each way, out in California. What are they thinking of in New York? Didn't they look at the map before they signed the contracts?"

Then slowly we had come to realize what great intrinsic work is behind booking a concert tour. Much as he may try, the manager cannot always line up the towns according to geography. The longer we were on the road, the more we admired, and the less we complained. . . .

The regular hum of the motor was relaxing. Silence descended on the bus, and I leaned back in my seat. My mind went back a few years to those early tours when the bus had been a panting, old-fashioned monster and our per capita expense allotment $1.50 per night; to the days when Rupert and Johanna had still been with us, and Johannes had occupied a crib in the rear of the bus; to the times when the driver had been—not Dave, but Frenchy, who lectured to us on America; then Tex, who knew the Don Cossacks and the Vienna Choir Boys; then Rudi, a big man with a heart as big as himself.

Lorli and Illi in those years, had been absent for a while —entrusted to a boarding school in the Bronx. That was before I had discovered the correspondence courses of the Calvert School in Baltimore. One writes the school, indicating the grade for which material is needed, and in a neat package arrives work for the whole school year, complete with pencil and paper. So our two chatterboxes had returned to us, and for all subsequent tours the family could stay together. After their "graduation" we had continued the method with Johannes.

With Johannes . . . a sudden thought, born of my meditations, brought me bolt upright in my seat.

"Listen, everyone," I remarked to the family at large, "shouldn't there be a meeting of the School Board?"

Johannes pretended not to hear. "Johannes is a lucky boy to be able to go to school in the bus," said Lorli loudly and significantly. No answer.

The School Board met. Long experience had taught us to organize quickly, and it was soon decided that I should be Superintendent of School; that Father Wasner would teach Latin and Divinity; that Agathe would be Professor of English and Maria of Mathematics. Rosmarie and Martina would be the Department of Fine Arts. Hedwig would give Manual Training and Spelling. Lorli was to teach History. Only Werner remained. He was unanimously voted Janitor.

As the School Board dispersed, Johannes, who had been standing beside Dave, felt an arm looped around his neck. Maria lassoed him and drew him firmly to the rear of the bus to consider the mysteries of Algebra. Thus school opened and the fall term began.

Fairhaven, Vermont. The bus rumbled up a perilously steep

slope, bumped wildly over a railroad track, climbed further, descended, and headed on to Granville. Across from me Father Wasner had finished his prayers and was reading *War and Peace*. Father prefers books of that length. One year he was deeply moved by Dostoevski's *The Idiot*—so moved that when a Russian friend, whom he had not seen for some months, appeared shortly afterwards at Cor Unum, Father greeted him with open arms and the words, "My dear Doctor, since I have read *The Idiot* I understand you much better!"

Suddenly, Dave sounded three long blasts of the horn— our ceremonial for the crossing of a State line. "So long, Vermont," we chorused, *"Auf Wiedersehen!"* With our arrival in New York State, Johannes changed "classrooms" to have a spelling lesson with Hedwig. Their voices sounded over the hum of the wheels.

"Spell 'vociferous.' "

"V-o-c-i-f-e-r-o-u-s."

"Good. Now what does it mean?"

Johannes coldly: "You ought to know. You are a girl."

"All right." Hedwig chose to overlook the comment. "Here's a word for men. Try 'voracious.' "

No answer. For a time there was silence in the bus. Then once again the student's voice was heard—this time from another quarter:

" 'Fourscore and seven years ago, our forefathers . . .' Lorli, that's stupid. It should be four *scores*. And who ever heard of having four *fathers?*"

I wondered myself.

Johannes continued, " '. . . our fore*fathers* brought forth upon this continent . . . upon this continent . . .' uh, say, I smell something wonderful!"

I had not realized that lunchtime could come so soon. In the rear of the bus, Maria was busily arranging a royal picnic: cold Wiener Schnitzel with potato and cucumber salad; celery and raw carrot sticks as an appetizer; and Linzer Torte for dessert. The hot coffee out of thermos bottles was served with whipped cream from home.

Somehow some cream landed on Hedwig's shoe.

"I'm sorry," said Johannes.

The words reminded me of something in the past.

It was on our second concert tour in America. The bus was waiting in front of the hotel. It was time to leave and the driver had already blown the horn several times; but, once again, a few of us were late—and I among them. When we finally sauntered out of the door, chatting gaily, and climbed casually into the bus, we met an icy atmosphere, a few caustic remarks—and then, all of a sudden, things happened. Everybody said something; and, when everybody said something again, it was in a higher key. Words flew around. Faces grew red, and eyes flashed. The whole storm had blown up so fast that afterwards no one could quite remember who had said the first word.

Then the Captain, my husband, stood up. Firmly, he commanded: "Everybody sit down and be quiet." We sat down. After a few moments, he spoke again, quietly. "Now, everybody say 'I'm sorry.'" Suddenly we were all very sorry indeed. Then the Captain drew us together around him to explain something that, in his days of circling the globe in a four-master, was called a *Tropenkoller*—a sudden flare-up of temperament that can occur easily when the same group of people has to live closely together for any length of time. He told us to be on our guard against the time when we could not stand the very sight of our neighbor. "Little things can drive us crazy," said my husband, "but if we watch out for them and are careful, flare-ups like the one this morning can usually be avoided."

How often we thought back on his words, and how right he was. The very fact that a group of people must live so closely together, sitting for seven to eight hours every day in the same small space, unable to get away, can create certain tensions. Everyone has his own little peculiarities. One might slouch in her seat; another might clear her throat "much too often"; a third might "always" look as though she had just got out of bed; another might fall asleep at the most inopportune moments and expect the rest to stop talking.

If hotels are noisy and we haven't slept enough, someone—
anyone—can get on our nerves.

There was many a storm during our life on wheels, with
thunder and lightning, often also with tears—tears of wrath
or tears of "nobody understands me"—and, finally, tears of
repentance. We all know that deep down we love each other
truly and that there is nothing one would not do for another.

After the coffee hour, everyone settled back for a short rest.
Carefully I looked over the "must-read" books in my satchel
and thoughtfully selected one: *How to Reduce, or Calorie-
Counting in Comfort*. Then I, too, relaxed for a nap.

By mid-afternoon the routine had resumed. Johannes was
invited to take his seat next to Father Wasner for a Religion
class. Hester came over to me, and we began working on the
piles of correspondence that had collected unanswered in the
last busy days before the departure.

"Dear Mrs. X.," I began, "Thank you for your letter . . ."

From across the aisle came: "First: Thou shalt . . . ; Second: Thou shalt . . ."

Lorli and Illi began to wind wool—obviously for their Christmas knitting. I saw Hedwig check quickly to make sure that
no one in the bus was sleeping. Then, with a "Don't worry,
it's only me," she fell to with her leather punch. That meant
future pocketbooks and book covers—also for Christmas. From
the rear came a persistent rasping sound. Werner had begun his silverwork. His specialty is making beautiful brooches
and pendants out of old silver coins, and the initial sand-
papering could always be done in the bus. Martina was
sketching—the design seemed to be a Canadian maple leaf. Of
course—a present for Jean. In front of me, Agathe sucked
thoughtfully on a pencil, getting ideas for the Christmas cards
she would soon cut in linoleum.

"Dear Mr. Z.," I continued, "In reply to your letter . . ."
. . . "Dear Mr. F. . . . After receiving your inquiry . . ."

"Thou shalt . . . Thou shalt not . . ."

Scrape. Punch. Scrape. Punch.

"Dear Mr. B. . . ."

We were well down into New York State when Father Wasner called the afternoon rehearsal. "What can you possibly have to rehearse," someone once asked us, "if you sing the same program every night?" Well, that's just it. Those who sing the same program from day to day must beware of the little irregularities that can creep in—so, frequently, we reviewed all our songs, even the best-known ones, singing them through very slowly, music in hand. Besides, there were new songs for every season, so that each fall tour meant careful rehearsal of unfamiliar carols and arrangements. *Old Black Joe* will always remind me of the Laurentian Mountains in Canada where we first practiced it. We learned *Nanita Nana* between Framingham and Boston. *Pastores ad Belém* makes me think less of Bethlehem than of endless cornfields in Illinois; and *In the Bleak Midwinter* suggests, of all things, the Florida orange groves.

On this particular day Father handed us the beautiful old carol, *Joy to the World*. The fervent simplicity of the melody had always appealed to us. Over and over we sang it—down the highways and across the bridges until the skyscrapers of New York came into view. As Dave brought the great bus into the heart of the city, we were still singing:

"Joy to the World! The Lord is come.
Let earth receive her King."

For a moment, as at the beginning of every tour, the sight of New York made me nervous, but quickly I dismissed the feeling. My answer seemed to well up in the very words we were singing:

"Joy to the World! The Saviour reigns.
Let men their songs employ!"

I knew—we all knew—that music can be a bond, a mission, drawing families, even nations, into common understanding.

With a sigh of contentment, I watched Dave wheel the great bus to a stop in front of the Hotel Wellington and saw the face of the doorman break into a smile of recognition and welcome. In a few moments we would all be inside; and while Hester checked in for us at the desk, we would hastily purchase a copy of *Cue* magazine to plan our free evening in New York. Quickly we all collected overnight belongings and began to put on our jackets.

In the front of the bus Dave stood up to stretch. "What are the orders for tomorrow, Father?" he asked. And, as we stepped down to greet the smiling faces of Al, Ray, Benny, and John, our bellboy friends, Father Wasner made the last general announcement of the day:

"Tomorrow: rehearsal at three. Day after tomorrow: nine o'clock rolling!"

3

The Town Hall Concert

We were not really "on wheels" in 1940, the year we sang our first Christmas concerts in Town Hall. It seems far back in the past now—Johannes was not quite two. Just the same, even across the years, none of us can forget how nervous we all felt when our manager, F. C. Schang, told us that Columbia Concerts had taken Town Hall for the two Sundays before Christmas—for the Trapp Family Singers.

It was not that we felt self-conscious about appearing on a concert stage. After a season of concerts here and there, we were beginning to know what to expect. We had come to realize that a good concert manager is born, not made—with strong nerves, with a good sense of humor, with a rare combination of virtues—and that Freddy Schang had them all; but, for all our confidence in Freddy, we were nervous.

At our home which was then in Merion, Pennsylvania, we began long rehearsals early in August. As I have already told in *The Story of the Trapp Family Singers*, our concert program had been worked out to combine, in the first groups, sacred music with madrigals, and with music for the recorder, spinet and viola da gamba. Then, after a short intermission, during which we changed into our native Austrian dress, we would sing Austrian mountain songs and folk songs of all nations. Now, for these important Town Hall concerts, Maria was given a seventeenth-century pastorale for recorders. Father Wasner introduced us to Buxtehude's Christmas cantata, *In Dulci Jublio*, and surprised us with several motets of rare beauty. We began to feel fairly confident about the first half of the program, but the second half, which would be devoted entirely to carols, still bothered us. Everyone felt it should be done in some manner special to the occasion, yet no one could say just how.

It was Werner who finally came up one day with a practical suggestion. "Couldn't we sit around a table," he said, "the way the English Singers did?" The English Singers—how frequently Freddy had referred to this famous vocal group, "his group" in days gone by. A quick family poll revealed unanimous patriotic feeling that where England had succeeded, Austria should not fall behind. We would, of course, sing around a table. And—this was my husband's idea—we would bring our own Austrian Christmas Eve to the stage, with our table lighted only by the flame of an Advent candle, symbol of the Light of the World.

Martina had the next suggestion: "*Hirten auf um Mitternacht!* Couldn't we show how Papa sings *Hirten auf um Mitternacht* when he wakens us for Midnight Mass, and how we all join in one by one?"

Next Lorli—trust little Lorli—saw her advantage and quickly asked for a "real Christmas tree with real cookies."

At the mention of cookies, we suddenly heard from the youngest member of our family. He was a man of few words that year, but they were American and to the point. "O.K.," said Johannes.

So, little by little, it was decided. First, we would come onto a darkened stage, carrying our burning candles and enact the little scene. Then we would sit around the table and, as we began the carols, the lights on the Christmas tree would go on.

"Say," said Maria one day, "how are people going to know what this is all about?" So an explanation became necessary. I can still hear my own voice in Merion, nervously rehearsing the short speech I was to give: "Around eight o'clock, the house is dark and silent. The first one to get up is the father.

He comes down into the hall in his heavy winter coat, carrying a lighted lantern and singing a Christmas carol heard only once a year. . . . Everyone who hears him comes down also with his lantern, and there they stand, singing one verse after the other, each verse a tone higher, until the whole family is together. And then they go out in ice and snow to Midnight Mass—" How many, many times through the years I have made that little speech—so often that anyone of the old-timers in the audience could rise up today to prompt me if I forgot. But that year I worked over every word.

I remember that my husband made a special trip from Philadelphia to New York; and, at Abercrombie and Fitch, he bought collapsible storm lanterns fitted for candles. In September the girls put last-minute touches to our concert dresses—white silk skirts to the floor, black and gold damask bodices, a red rose for each. Agathe turned out fresh ruffles and blouses for everyone; and Hedwig, our cobbler, made the gold sandals shine. Thumps and bangs and much hammering came from the carpenter shop while the boys worked on a little blue Tyrolean chair for Johannes, who was to sit beside me during the carols. Martina painted a bright Tyrolean design on the finished product—and we left for the preliminary concerts of our fall tour with the gay decoration hardly dry.

At long last the great day came. The first Town Hall concert was set for 5:30 P.M.—and I almost didn't get there.

Suddenly, at noon, with all my heart, I had wanted real Christmas candles on the Christmas tree, and New York hadn't known I was going to want them. A kind sales lady in Saks Fifth Avenue suggested that I try "Eighty-sixth Street around the German quarter," and somehow I ended up in a subway marked "Coney Island." To make things worse, a little girl seated next to me looked curiously at my Austrian dress and asked, "Are you a gypsy?"

I knew that I must, mu-u-st find my way back to Town Hall, and my cause became a public affair. "Town Hall?" said

the man next to me. "Say, Leddy, whassa madda? You coulda
tooka cab at Moitle Street."

A big fellow in overalls spoke up, "C'mon, Leddy, I'm
seein' ya inda right caw."

My poor English! I resolved firmly, once the concerts were
over, to plunge into lesson seventeen of my grammar book.
With gestures, I thanked my kind friends, left the subway,
and took a taxi. I arrived at five-ten. My children were frantic,
but the tree on the stage was beautifully and completely
trimmed. (Hedwig had bought the candles in a ten-cent store
near the Wellington.)

I was whisked into my concert dress, and we began. The
hall was filled to capacity, and the audience seemed warm
and appreciative. Motets, pastorale, the Buxtehude—everything appeared to go well. During the intermission, as we
changed into Austrian costumes, our excitement mounted.
Would the candles stay upright in the lanterns? Would there
be chairs to go round? Would the lights be dimmed at the
right moment? And—as a major problem—would Johannes be-
have on the stage? Every two minutes someone repeated his
instructions to him, as he stood in his little blue suit in the
dressing room: he was to come on-stage carrying his blue chair,
sit down next to me, and stay seated. Johannes looked like
an angel with his golden hair and round blue eyes, as he solemnly heard his directions, but . . . well, every family has
its uncertainties.

Yet everything seemed to go according to plan. I made the
announcement; and, as I came backstage, the lights were
properly dimmed. From the wings, Father Wasner's voice
began the deep strong notes of the familiar Christmas call:

> "Hirten auf um Mitternacht,
> Erhebt euch aus dem Schlafe!"

Next the boys joined in, coming from the other side:

> "Auf, der gute Hirte wacht . . ."

Then, one by one, came the sopranos and altos:

"Eilt zu Maria, zum Kripplein geschwind!
*Kommet und grüsset das göttliche Kind!"**

Last of all, I brought Johannes in. One little hand was holding tight to mine, the other clutched his gay blue chair. We all reached our places safely; and, after having sung verse after verse, each one tone higher, we sat down around the table. With some technical difficulty, Johannes managed to put his chair next to mine and established himself upon it. At no point did he let go of my hand.

Father Wasner lit the great red candle in the middle of the table. The flame sprang up, and the candle glowed deep red. Behind us, the lights of the Christmas tree were turned on as we sang our first carol. To our surprise, there was no applause. A few faint claps followed the second and third. "What-is-wrong?" I telegraphed to Father. He signaled back: "Don't-worry-they're-afraid-they-aren't-supposed-to." We were disappointed, though we could feel the sympathy of the audience. Johannes became interested in the flame of one of the lanterns. As his golden head bent dangerously over it, I tugged firmly on the hand in mine. The next two songs went less well.

Finally we reached the Tyrolean *Virgin's Lullaby,* an alto solo with humming accompaniment. I turned to explain to the audience: "When the Blessed Mother saw her little Son, her heart was so overflowing with love for Him that she had to put it into words, and she sang to Him:

'Thy little cheeks—how red they are,
Thy little mouth—sweetly it smiles.

* "Shepherds, up, your watch to take!
  Your time of sleep is ending,
  For the Good Shepherd is awake,
  His earthly flock attending.
  Haste to the Manger, to Mary so mild,
  Come and adore Him, the Heavenly Child!"
  —Translation from: F. Wasner, ed., *The Trapp Family Book of Christmas Songs,* Pantheon Books, Inc.

Oh, how I love Thee,
My Child and my God.'

And all the angels in Heaven came to join her, singing."
Looking down at my son's golden head, I began the song,

"'*Deine Wangelen*
Seind rös'le rot
I will di liab'n
Bis in den Tod.'"

The melody of *The Virgin's Lullaby* is meditative, grave,
and tender. The music casts a spell. As it floated out into the
audience, we could feel their rapt listening.

"'*In deine Wangelen*
Seind Grüabele drein.'"

Behind me there was a thud. An apple had fallen from the
tree.

"'*Du bischt und bleibscht*
Ja ewig mein . . .'"*

Suddenly, Johannes let go of my hand and left his chair.
With waddling baby steps and a solemnity that in no way
detracted from the mood of the song, he crossed the stage,
picked up the apple, and returned to his place. As we sang
the second verse and the third, he slid his little hand in mine.

"'*I will di liab'n*
Bis in dem Tod . . .'"

Tremendous applause, which was not exactly directed to
the singers, followed the last notes!
Quietly then we rose from our chairs. In German we sang

* "In Thy cheeks aglow
  Are dimples fine.
  Thou art and shalt
  Be ever mine."
—Translation from: Maria Augusta Trapp, *Around the Year with
the Trapp Family*, Pantheon Books, Inc.

one verse of our favorite Austrian *Stille Nacht*, with its world-message of peace. The second verse we sang in English. Still humming the melody, we picked up our lanterns, crossed the stage, and filed through the doors on either side. As the last notes ended, the stage was empty and the curtains came together. Our first Town Hall Christmas concert was over.

There were many curtain calls, and the next day an enthusiastic press, then letters of congratulation. We were deeply moved, very grateful, very happy. Could we have known it then, the joy was just beginning. (I wonder how many hundreds of thousands of people have left us, after a concert, with the sound of *Stille Nacht* in their ears and its message in their hearts?) *Deine Wangelen, The Virgin's Lullaby*, has been sung after weddings, and before baptisms; in winter, in summer, on four different continents. So many times, since those first Town Hall concerts—so many times, through so many States and in so many countries, the "Family on Wheels" has been privileged to bring Christmas to the hearts of its audience. . . .

4

All About Concerts

The audience. Dear, wonderful, unpredictable audience! To begin any concert was always, for us, a constantly new experience. The curtains parted, we took a bow, and we looked down into a sea of people who, for the next two hours, would be our musical guests. Sometimes we could distinguish the faces of old friends—in Jordan Hall, Boston, we always looked for the Scoborias and Edith Smith; in Town Hall, as the years went by, we knew just where to find Mrs. Bender, Mrs. Dana, Kathleen O'Brien, Emma Diehl and all the other smiling old-timers from our Music Camp. More often than not, though, and especially in the small towns, we sang to complete strangers, to a conglomeration of people from different walks of life—of different ages and interests, with each individual heart and mind filled with its own ideas.

The curtains would open. There was brief applause, then an expectant stillness settling over the hall. Sometimes it took a little while to establish a rapport with the audience. In fact, there were certain occasions that called for considerable will power on our part. I shall never forget a concert in Alabama with young children in the first row. We had just reached the *Kyrie Eleison* in Palestrina's *Missa Brevis*, when a round-eyed little boy, looking up at us thoughtfully and dreamily, engaged one stubby forefinger in an intent exploration of his nasal passages. I couldn't help watching him out of the corner of my eye. He worried me, but next to him, his sister worried me more, and I was right. Suddenly, before I could call out,

"Don't!", she discovered what he was doing and slapped the naughty little hand. The result was a completely off-key howl in the first row.

After the *Kyrie* comes the *Agnus Dei*, one of the greatest pieces of choral literature. At the end of the first row, a second little girl had the marvelous idea of rolling up her program and using it for a telescope. The others caught on immediately, and suddenly we were looking at a whole front row of little star-gazers.

"So you give children's concerts," a dear lady once wrote to me. "How wonderful to sing for the flower of the nation!" If only she knew how many times we felt like magicians, snake-charmers, and cross-country runners, racing at top speed to capture the attention of the "flower of the nation"—but truly, once they are won, there is nothing more thrilling than the heart-felt, emphatic, thundering applause of the young.

Sometimes, inevitably, the size of the hall would affect our ability to create a proper concert atmosphere. Jordan Hall, Town Hall, Orchestra Hall in Chicago, Constitution Hall in Washington—these are old friends built for music and dedicated to music; but the concert hall of any average town is usually the school auditorium, or even worse, the gymnasium, still filled with the aroma of a recent basketball game. Sometimes the "stage" has been improvised at one end, with a perilous ladder-like stair. Sometimes we found the audience sitting left and right, while we sang towards the empty wall opposite. More often than not our dressing rooms were locker rooms. Besides the gymnasiums, we have sung in churches where, whatever the other problems, the acoustics are magnificent; in hotel ballrooms where they definitely are not; in movie houses where usually there are no acoustics at all. Once, in the Canadian Middle West, we even sang in a skating rink with a seating capacity of seven thousand. The stage was a wooden platform in the middle—best reached by bicycle; and we needed binoculars to see our "audience," a heroic little group who, alone, had braved the town's worst downpour to be present. They sat huddled together some miles away from us, while behind our impromptu stage rain came pouring through the tin roof and made a big puddle on the sandy floor. Father Wasner's hands, conducting the songs, occasionally caught a fat raindrop.

Father Wasner is really Monsignor Wasner and has been since he was made a Papal Chamberlain in 1952, but the "Father" is very hard to drop. By vocation a priest and by nature a scholar, he is also a great musician, and far from an easy taskmaster. Martina once said, years ago, "Father Wasner is *two* people—a Father *and* a conductor." How often we have quoted her since. While in "private life" Father is quiet, good-natured, humble, unassuming, just let him begin a rehearsal and . . . "He doesn't even *look* the same," Martina complained. No, he doesn't. A steely quality comes into his eyes, and he turns into an uncompromising, relentless disciplinarian—to whom we remain utterly devoted, and for whose musical integrity and deep spirituality we will always be eternally grateful.

It was Father Wasner who, in those early days in Austria, really took our music and our program in hand. Before he came, we had had two reasons for singing; to praise God in our morning and evening services, and to enjoy the great beauty of folk songs as we found them in our hikes through the Tyrolean hills and valleys. With him, we discovered the intricate beauty of madrigals—the "home music" of the sixteenth and seventeenth centuries. He enlarged our modest collection of songs and helped us to study works which we never could have handled alone, though the range of choice stayed essentially the same: church music, folk music, home music—with recorder, spinet, and viola da gamba.

Before long we had worked up a repertoire of some two hundred numbers; and from these, when the time came for our American tours, we chose the best of the best, renewing and adding to them every year. There were always several programs for each season: one for the average public, one for schools, and one—more rarely sung—for the most serious music lovers. The first half of the program, as I have said, usually presented music of the old masters—sacred, secular and instrumental. Experience soon taught us to begin with canons and madrigals and end with sacred motets, since the audience is in a more receptive mood for understanding and appreciating profound and difficult works immediately before the intermission. During the second half of the program, we used many of Father Wasner's "American" choral arrangements, which have since been published and are widely used today, but we found it an uphill battle to make the American folk song known in its own right against popular hit tunes such as *Pistol Packin' Mama*. Even today, "hit" tunes affect the minds, the character, the emotional life of our growing children. Psychiatrists are raising their voices in warning, as jukeboxes, radio and television, going from dawn to dusk, help spread the poison of synthetic, artificial, rhythmical noise.

Perhaps I feel so deeply about this question, because I have seen the reactions of people thirsty for beauty, when they come to realize that beauty is to be had for the asking. Perhaps it is because, as I look back now, certain moments in our own musical experience stand out as especially breathtaking. Some of them are associated with the dear friends who, from time to time, joined our musical family. We will always remember Charlene Petersen's voice in *Early One Morning*, or Hal Petersen's trumpet solo in *Quem Pastores Laudavere*; or Virginia Farri and Donald Meissner singing Mozart's *Alma Dei Creatoris*. . . .

But this brings me back to what I originally started to say about "the audience." No matter what problems present themselves with the hall, the audience, or the weather, sooner or later for the concert artist comes the magic moment when "it" happens—when long rows of individuals in the audience are transformed little by little into a single, listening family; when all together—audience, singers, director, and music—become one feeling entity, held together in spirit for the short hours of their musical acquaintance; and, in a deeper sense, forever.

For us, the highlight of our whole life as a singing family was the concert we were privileged to give with the Philadelphia Orchestra in December, 1953. Father Wasner had orchestrated Franz Schubert's *The Lord Is My Shepherd* for the occasion. None of us can ever forget how the harps started the short prelude, then the string section took over; and finally for us, the singers, the sound became a luminous cloud coming closer and closer from behind until it reached us, reached the audience, included us all, and like a magic carpet, took us, singing, out of time and space into the realm of pure music.

How can we, all of us, best communicate a sense of beauty and the joy of singing to all "thirsty ones," and especially to all teen-agers, all jukebox fans, all lovers of rock 'n roll?

5

A *Quiz Program*

One wall of the dining room at Cor Unum is nearly covered by a tremendous map of the United States—the "map of our rolling," we called it. Usually, before leaving on a tour, we planned out our route with pins and a red thread so that the people at home could follow us from place to place. Then, between trips, all the pins came out and waited for a new itinerary.

During our Christmas vacation in 1948, just after Maria had stripped the map, we had among our ski guests at Cor Unum a Professor of Physics from a well-known New England university. When he learned, during the supper conversation, that we had sung more than fifteen hundred concerts in the United States, he suddenly invented a quiz program for the evening—something between "Stump the Experts," "Stop the Music," and "Information Please." He was to point to any town on the map. If we had sung there and could identify it, fine; if not, we would have to pay a forfeit.

Everyone agreed, and in high spirits we assembled around the map. Solemnly, the Professor took a knitting needle from Maria's basket and, using it as a pointer, he began: "Salem, Massachusetts?"

"Visit to the Pilgrims' Museum," Hedwig answered quickly. "And Mr. George Murphy arranged a most interesting trip through the city, and . . ."

"Thank you," said the Professor. "Iberia, Louisiana?"

Johannes' hand waved frantically.

"That's where we met the little boy who played in *Louisiana Story*," he volunteered, "and he showed us his raccoons!"

"Dayton, Ohio?"

We all chuckled, while Maria explained, "We sang there during the war; and, while we were giving the concert, the hotel sold our rooms. If it hadn't been for the friendly ladies of the local committee, who put us up in private homes, we would have had to sit up in the lobby!"

"Mitchell, South Dakota?"

"Corn Palace!" we chorused—remembering the multicolored corncobs that decorate the huge hall inside and out.

So far we were holding our own in the quiz. The Professor tried several more places: Escanaba, Michigan—with keen memories of our ride on a frozen lake that kept planning to unfreeze beneath us; then, Newton, Kansas. *The Story of the Trapp Family Singers* tells how that town generously offered its only wartime transportation—a hearse—to drive us to our train in Wichita. We rolled merrily off under cover singing (I think this was Lorli's idea), "Oh, bury me not on the lone prairie!"

"Van Nuys, California?"

Father Wasner answered feelingly for that one. During the Van Nuys concert a briefcase disappeared from his dressing room. Strangely enough, a letter it contained was dutifully mailed by the thief and reached him some six months later.

"Chicago?"

"You're getting too easy, Professor!" I told him. All our memories of Chicago would need an evening for themselves. Chicago—where our driver, Rudi, became annoyed to see a fur-coated lady leaving at the intermission of our concert. Firmly, he blocked her way in the lobby, turned her around by the shoulders, and said simply, "You are not going to leave yet! You'll miss the best part!" Not until we learned it the next day from her own good-humored comments in print, did we realize that Rudi had sent back into the hall none other than Claudia Cassidy, the well-known Chicago critic, whose enthusiastic or devastating write-ups could shape a reputation. . . .

Chicago—and my famous search-for-Mrs.-Saunders. For years during the war we had had a lively exchange of letters with a certain Father Saunders, American Army Chaplain in Salzburg, who helped tremendously in delivering packages sent to him from The Trapp Family Austrian Relief, Inc. Among other things, Father Saunders had written: "If you are ever in Chicago, please call Mother and greet her for me." To me, the name, Saunders, was completely unique; so at our next stop in Chicago, half an hour before leaving, I picked up the telephone book with great confidence. With a gulp, I realized that Father Saunders' dear mother was hidden somewhere among pages and pages of families by the same name. One eye on the clock, I asked for the first number. . . . "Hello, is there a Mrs. Saunders here who has a son who is an army chaplain?" . . . "Hello, is there a Mrs. Saunders here—" . . . "Hello, is there . . ." I did find her. She was number eighteen. If her husband's first name had been William or Zachary . . .

Three more rapid questions followed Chicago: Saginaw, Michigan—where the local train had kerosene lamps and a coal stove; Houston, Texas—and our first Stock Show; Livingston, Montana—"Where we ate our first buffalo steak," said Johannes distastefully.

The Professor decided next on a small, out-of-the-way spot: "Ely, Nevada?"

Ely, Nevada. "Mother, remember?" said Lorli significantly, and I remembered. Ely, Nevada, had given us our first glimpse of legal gambling. In my curiosity to see as many establishments as possible, I went in and out of saloons the whole length of the main street. At the same time, Lorli and Johannes were frantically looking for me for permission to spend the night in an abandoned silver mine. Afterwards, I learned that they had been right behind me, from one saloon to another, asking everyone, "Have you seen my mother—Mrs. Trapp, from the Trapp Family Singers?"

By now it was evident to all of us that our incredible quizluck could not go on much longer. Martina tried strategy.

"Professor," she called from her corner, "aren't you going to go into Canada at *all?*"

A great sound of laughter and some loud coughing greeted this question. Though Martina's engagement to a certain Canadian, Jean Dupire, had not yet been announced, the situation was becoming clearer day by day. "You couldn't *possibly* want the Professor to ask us about Montreal, could you?" asked Agathe. Martina's rosy smile showed that—yes, she possibly could.

The year we first sang in Montreal we had been told that the Salle Plateau would be our gateway into French Canada; and we felt very humbly glad to realize, at the end of the evening, that the gate was really wide open. Little did we know, however, that besides the musical success, this concert would have such far-reaching consequences. As we looked down from the stage, we must have seen several young men applauding wildly in the front row, although none of us could exactly remember them the following summer when, carrying their tents and knapsacks, they walked into the Trapp Family Music Camp. They had come for one weekend—Jean and Gabriel; Jacques, Jean and Pierrot; Jacques and Irénée. They stayed for a month and . . . well, Martina seemed quite satisfied.

The next question was: "Calgary, Alberta?" We should have paid a forfeit there because Calgary made us think more of Edmonton. The road was so icy on the night of the Edmonton concert that we left our bus in Calgary and took a train. Three derailed cars on the track ahead delayed us. The railroad company managed to get word of our trouble to Edmonton; and at 9:30 P.M., when we finally arrived, we found our audience still waiting, while a local pianist led them in singing. Everyone cheered and clapped as we entered and hurried directly to the stage. At 11:30 P.M. we were still singing. Then, just as hurriedly as we had come, we left—barely making the last train back down to Calgary.

"That was as close as we ever came to a real catastrophe," Lorli remarked, and her whole tone of voice implied: "Too bad we missed."

"What about St. Catherine, Ontario?" came a loud stage whisper from Johannes. It was true. The concert in St. Catherine had gone very well, but during the night came one of the worst snowstorms in the history of the town. There was no possible means of transportation, and the snowdrifts were almost impassable, even on foot. We had our usual concert luggage—and no boys, because it was wartime. Rupert and Werner were with the ski troops in Camp Hale, Colorado. We pushed, tugged, and pulled the spinet, recorders and suitcases—first to the Canadian border; then, at long last, past the cold frozen glitter of Niagara Falls and across the bridge to the State of New York. Only Johannes seemed to have the time of his life. . . .

By now the Professor appeared to be getting a little tired and was leaning against the map, with his spinal column somewhere in the vicinity of Utah. "I suppose," he said, "that no matter how deep the snow, your show always goes on, but what happens if one of you gets sick?"

So often we have been asked that question. Several times I have been desperately sick and had to miss an entire tour, while Hedwig carried on gallantly for me; and, when the children were small, we went through everything. In Washington, we had the measles; in Boston, the chicken-pox; and in Texas, the mumps. Measles and chicken-pox could be handled quite easily—my husband stayed behind with the sick child. As fast as one rejoined the group, another came down; so Georg would sit in a new hotel, patiently reading the same fairy tales to the next invalid. But with mumps—well, Johannes started it, and within a few days four of us had picked up the germ. There was nothing to do but to retire to a cabin court in Wichita Falls, Texas, for an unexpected week of rest, which the non-invalids spent singing and dancing to the music of Maria's accordion, while our frantic manager canceled concerts for us in Florida and Cuba.

For the Professor's benefit, however, I particularly mentioned what had happened at our first concert in Madison, Wisconsin. We had left Johannes in bed in the hotel with a rather nasty cold, and under the care of Martha, a school friend of Maria's. During the intermission, in the half-second just before curtain time, a bellboy from the hotel came panting up to me with: "Your little boy has a fever of a hundred and five. The lady wants to know if she should call a doctor." I could only gasp out a hurried "Yes, of course—immediately," when the curtains opened and we bowed smilingly to the assembled audience. After our last encore, the doctor was waiting for me backstage. Johannes had pneumonia. He and Martha finally caught up with us a few weeks later in Saint Joseph, Missouri. Years later, I told our quiz-master, we sang again in Madison, and the same doctor, who still fondly remembered the little blue-eyed boy, was at the concert for a touching meeting of old friends. . . .

By this time it was getting late, and we knew that in the chapel above us the bell would soon ring for Benediction; but the little group around the "rolling-map" was still bursting with helpful suggestions: "Mother, tell about Brunswick, Maine, where Illi got a live mouse in the mail on April first."

"What about Pennsylvania, where Papa skidded on the ice and ran into a telegraph pole—and we drove through Pittsburgh in half a car. . . ."

"How about Southern Pines and the Advent wreath we made in the woods?"

"How about Rapid City?"

"Tell about Johannes in Saint Louis, Missouri." . . .

I tried to sort out a few answers. In Rapid City, South Dakota, Charlene and Hal Petersen had had the generous but fatal idea of taking me to see *Cyrano de Bergerac* at the local cinema. I wept right straight through and came out of the theatre completely exhausted. As Charlene and Hal led me back to the hotel, I walked blindly between them, sobbing bitterly, "Why didn't he *tell* her? Why didn't he? Now it's too late. He's dead."

The elevator girl expressed her sincere sympathy, and soon it was all over the hotel that someone in the Trapp Family had died.

When Johannes was three or four years old, we sang a concert in Saint Louis, Missouri, on March nineteenth, the Feast of St. Joseph. The Sisters of Saint Joseph, who were sponsoring the concert, had of course celebrated the feast day with particular solemnity. Backstage during the intermission, one of them said to Johannes, "Isn't it too bad that you don't know a hymn in honor of Saint Joseph, dear . . . you could have sung it today."

Johannes' round blue eyes looked up at her, and we heard him say, "We do have one."

"Do you, dear!" answered the Sister. "Now, what is it?" And with every Trapp Family ear anxiously listening:

"*Old Black Joe*," said Johannes.

And . . . and . . . and . . . There were so many other things to tell. I would have loved to explain to the Professor all about how, in South Carolina, we had picked pine boughs to make our Advent wreath; and how, in Virginia, we had hung it in the bus; how, inside the bus, we followed the liturgical seasons as faithfully as the wheels of the bus followed the road. I wanted to explain to him that it didn't make any difference whether we were out west in the Mojave Desert or driving through the plains of Nebraska, or caught in the ice of northern Canada—that, as long as we were together, living and celebrating together, the bus had turned into a home; and we knew that two things—our music and our tradition of family life—were permanent treasures which together, or separately, we would always carry with us. But it was too late that night to begin.

"And the rest is for another time," I said.

"All right," the Professor agreed, "but just give me one last question." Peering intently at the map, he came out with his final selection, "Springfield."

There was a short silence. Then, as with one voice, we all cried, "*Which* Springfield?"—while Lorli explained: "We have sung in Springfield, Massachusetts; Springfield, Vermont; Springfield, Ohio; Springfield, Illinois; and Springfield, Missouri."

Above the general laughter, in which our Professor most heartily joined, came the ringing of the chapel bell.

6

The Old America

Over and over during our first months in America letters from friends and relatives in Europe kept repeating the same question: "Tell us all about the Indians—the Indian braves!" Bitter was their disappointment when we had to write home to them that we had not seen in the streets of New York or Philadelphia so much as one live Indian—brave or otherwise.

We did come across many Indian names during our first tours: Niagara, Narragansett, Saratoga, Chautauqua, Canajoharie. Lorli and Illi started their own collection of more practical words, such as "chipmunk," "succotash," "skunk." I remember that as baby Johannes slept in his crib in the rear of the bus, I used to sing him a lullaby made up of such names as Shinnecock, Susquehanna, Winnipesaukee and Chattanooga.

Then finally, in the course of our travels, we came to meet and know Indian tribes from all over the United States, so that we could write back to Europe about the Seminoles, the Navajos, the Zunis; about saintly little Kateri Tekawitha of the Mohawks. In northeast Maine, near Old Town, an Indian ferryman took us, on an old-fashioned picture-book ferry, over to an island inhabited by the Penobscot tribe. There we admired their beautiful sweet-grass baskets, and I made the mistake of leaving a down payment for a shipment of baskets in various sizes, colors, and shapes to be used as Christmas presents. Two months later no baskets had arrived —only a letter from one of the Indian ladies.

"How much money did you give my nephew?" she wrote. "He hasn't been sober since you left!"

In New Mexico, we visited the old pueblo village of Acoma. The idea of doing this had occurred to us during one of our Western tours as we crossed the flat sandy plain near Laguna. We had just been reading Willa Cather's *Death Comes for the Archbishop*, with its Book Three: "Mass at Acoma"; and the dry red plain was just as she describes it, all plateaus and bumpy pillars of rock—a country pulled by the wind and blown by the sand, "still waiting to be made into a landscape." In the far distance, on the great rock of Acoma, we could make out the white outline of the pueblo and the spiky towers of an old Mexican church. It so happened that we had a free day between concerts in Albuquerque and Santa Fe. Suddenly, we wanted to visit the village. . . .

There is no resident priest in Acoma. The church there is kept locked now; and in Laguna the Franciscan Father who had the key tried very hard to discourage us from going there. "Acoma Indians are not at all friendly towards tourists," he warned. "You might not see a single one, or else— They are even known to be quite rough with white people."

"But, Father," we protested, "we are not tourists. They are Americans, and so are we. We want to celebrate Holy Mass there tomorrow for everyone."

There was a long silence. Then, "All right," said the Father, "I'll get you the key to the church." But he looked worried.

Early the next morning we set out. It was the third of February and the Feast of St. Blaise. The sun was bright, but the air was cold, and it was windy; around us the lonely rocks, the flat sandy plain seemed bare and empty. From time to time fat fistfuls of sand blew against our windshield, as though some old world poltergeist were trying to blind us or turn us back. The highway became a dirt road winding through gritty tangles of brush, until finally we reached the foot of the Acoma mesa, the great rock on which the Indians had built their pueblo.

There was no one in sight. With Father Wasner ahead, we

started single file up the steep path. We passed a heap of bright-colored pottery and some fresh-chopped wood, but a strange empty silence seemed to hang over the great rock. The top of the mesa, too, was cold and empty. Not one living soul was to be seen anywhere; not even the barking of a dog or the cackling of a chicken could be heard. Even the great church of Acoma, rising like a fortress from the steep table-rock, was silent, closed, wrapped in its own waiting. As Father put the rusty key into the rusty lock, we turned to look back over the empty village. There was no one in sight.

Slowly, as the key turned, the huge door creaked open, and a cold square of sunlight broke the dusty shadows of the silent nave. Father went to look for the sacristy. Hedwig and Maria climbed far up into the steeple and rang the bell—a deep, powerful bell whose rusty voice rang out over the village and down, down, down into the desert. . . .

Gathered at the foot of the altar, we started to recite together the beautiful opening prayers of the Mass. "*Introibo ad altare Dei,*" Father began. ("I will go in unto the altar of God.")

"*Ad Deum qui laetificat juventutem meam,*" we answered.

"*Judica me, Deus, et discerne causam meam . . .*" the prayers continued, rising up to join the old, old echoes of other prayers in other years. . . . Suddenly, there were footsteps behind us. We struggled not to look around.

"*Emitte lucem tuam, et veritatem tuam . . .*" Father continued. ("Send out Thy light and Thy truth. They have led me and brought me unto Thy holy hill.") The door creaked, opened wider, creaked again. There were more footsteps behind us, the shuffling sound of many moccasins on an earthen floor.

Did we only dream it—or were our answering voices really joined by others?

"And Thy people shall rejoice in Thee."

The whole church seemed suddenly filled to its broken roof-beams with one great cry of response.

At the end, when the Holy Sacrifice of the Mass was over, we saw them. They were everywhere. The huge church was

nearly filled with them in their quaintly patterned blankets
and bandannas. Here and there one of them wore a bright
feather thrust into his hair. The women had brought small
babies tied to their backs. Silently, with great dignity and
regal simplicity of bearing, they stood there, watching the
altar, watching Father Wasner, watching us.

Then Father, instead of leaving the altar, took two steps
forward. "Dear friends in Acoma," he said very slowly and
simply, "today is the Feast of St. Blaise, a very holy bishop
who once during his lifetime saved a little boy from choking.
That is why the Church today gives the blessing of Saint
Blaise against sickness of the throat and all other evils. Anyone who wants to receive the blessing may come forward."

One at a time, with the same silent dignity, the Indians
came up to kneel at the foot of the altar while Father Wasner,
holding two blessed candles crosswise in front of each dark-
skinned throat, gave the blessing. Some of them came up
twice. Some, with much difficulty, brought in a barrel of water
to be blessed, while others ran off to get vessels from home,
and women filled the dry font at the entrance to the church.

Then, and only then, did one of them speak. The Chief,
an elderly man with a feather in his gray hair, stepped forward and addressed us in the beautiful poetic language of the
Acoma Indians which, for our benefit, his official interpreter
translated into English. He thanked us for singing, he thanked
Father Wasner for having offered Holy Mass in their church
and for having blessed them all. Then, with great warmth and
the same indefinable dignity, he invited our family to join
with his family as members of the tribe of Acoma Indians.
Deeply moved, as much by the invitation as by the haunting,
mysterious sadness in their beautiful eyes, we accepted their
invitation.

After the Chief had addressed us, he turned to his own
people and in a touching ceremony himself distributed the
holy water according to families. When everyone had received
his share, we all left the church together . . . and then followed a wonderful hour. Every single family wanted to receive us. The older Indians spoke no English; but the younger

ones, who had gone to American schools, interpreted for them. In the babble of voices, while they told us of the rain and farming problems, Father went from door to door, blessing each home and visiting the sick. Lorli and Rosmarie were soon racing like monkeys up and down the ladders of the three-story pueblo houses with the native children who showed them around. "Breakfast" appeared—a great basket of fresh bread which an old Indian lady brought, still hot, from the round clay baking-ovens at one side of the village. Tactfully, on the other side of the cliff, someone pointed out the rather primitive "powder rooms." Finally, with great solemnity, we were taken to a closed building consisting of four walls with no door or window, the interior reachable only by a ladder through the roof. "This," said the Chief with particular emphasis, "is our kiva."

("And then we went down into the kiva," we later told our Franciscan Father in Laguna. He jumped as if stung.

"That's not possible!" he said. Only then did we fully appreciate that we had seen something no tourist ever gets to see. The kiva, for the Pueblo Indians, is their innermost sanctuary, the last bit of privacy which they anxiously and jealously keep for themselves and do not share with the white man. The Chief had really meant what he said in the church. We "belonged.")

We stayed till the latest possible minute. Then, accompanied by the entire tribe, we walked to the edge of the cliff where the steep path leads down. It was a lingering goodbye. Many times we turned round, and I can still see that picture: against the deep blue sky on the rim of the steep mesa, the Indians—*our* Indians—in their colorful blankets and bandannas, with their long straight hair blowing in the wind and their sad eyes following us down; then, behind them and high above, the great church of Acoma, the fortress of God, with its thick adobe walls glowing deep yellow in the noonday sun.

Many years have passed since we traveled back that day over the flat red plain to our concert in Santa Fe; but never, no matter where we are, could any one of us today receive the blessing of Saint Blaise on the third of February without saying, with our lips or with our hearts, "*Et cum fratribus nostris absentibus*—and with our absent brethren in Acoma. Amen."

7

The New America

Acoma stands out today as a chapter apart in the years when we "discovered America." As I have already said, we quickly learned that Indian braves were not to be found on every street corner; and—for a while, at least—we began to conclude that everything in America is big, busy, commercial and in-a-hurry.

All kinds of first impressions worked to convince us: elevators and subways and escalators, for instance; or the sign we saw on a dangerous curve outside Boston: "Why go on living if we can bury you for fifty dollars?" When Maria first heard that New York has over three million telephones, she could only say, "What if they all rang at once?"; and, in the London Terrace super-market, I spent all my money buying up "giant economy" sizes. We had a hard time getting used to publicity methods that made it necessary to trim a Christmas tree in August because there must be pictures in December; and we could not quite understand why concert singers must be "sold" or "bought," but through it all, we felt that in some way we were becoming more American.

Early trips with the bus helped to educate us—especially the first one, which nearly gave poor Frenchy a nervous breakdown. It was a great day when we rolled away from the Wellington, through the Holland Tunnel, and out over the Pulaski Skyway.

In no time at all, we encountered samples of American roadside advertising. First came a giant billboard urging us

to drink Coca-Cola. Frenchy stopped the bus while I took
a picture.

We were hardly back on the highway again when I heard
the family reciting in chorus:

> "No lady wants
> To dance or dine
> Together with
> A porcupine—
> Burma Shave."

Frenchy stopped the bus.

We passed a large factory. Frenchy stopped.

Next it was a clover-leaf turn and six road signs on top of
one another; after that, a filling station with two sets of
pumps. Each time, Frenchy stopped. Late in the afternoon
(we were back on the highway again after having driven off
for hamburgers in a diner), Lorli's high voice suddenly exclaimed, "Look—a graveyard! An auto graveyard!" We were
passing a hillside covered with rusty carcasses that Americans
"had just thrown away."

"Frenchy, stop!" came the familiar cry and, camera in hand,
I rose purposefully from my seat. Just as purposefully,
Frenchy stepped firmly on the gas.

"Tell your mother," he said over his shoulder to Rupert,
"that if we have to stop at every junk heap to take a picture,
she can drive!"

Bit by bit auto graveyards and billboards lost their interest
as the wheels of the bus, crossing and recrossing the nation,
brought us closer to the heart of things. At the heart of
things, oddly enough, we encountered prejudice. In certain
places our Austrian clothes made us suspected and mistrusted.
In others, local churchgoers looked at us with some doubt.
Catholics in America are Irish, Italian, Polish, German, but
Austrian . . . ? Not until years later, when Father Saunders
called us his "O'Trapps" did we feel that the issue had been
in some way solved.

Then Frenchy and the bus took us to the Deep South. In

Austria we had once met a Negro—only one—a big, broad-shouldered bell-captain in an exclusive hotel in Vienna, and we had looked on him with reverence and awe as "the" colored man. Now we were driving through South Carolina in cotton-picking time; and for me *Uncle Tom's Cabin* came alive. This was truly the New World!

The next day we found out that the New World was newer than we had thought. We encountered "white" and "colored" rest rooms, "white" and "colored" waiting rooms, "white" and "colored" seats in public buses. For a while we simply drew our own conclusions. "Here in the South," we told ourselves, "colored people are at home. They choose to stay somewhat apart, and we must respect their privacy." So we resolved to watch the signs and not to disturb the native people if we could help it. But "colored" and "white" churches seemed to carry the question a little far. "Before God there is no difference," we thought, "so why shouldn't we all be together?" I had by then become used to Frenchy's mumbling, so I did not really listen to what he had to say when Rosmarie kissed one of her new little friends goodbye as we entered the bus. . . .

But all too soon we found out the truth. After a Sunday Mass somewhere in Georgia, the parish priest paid us a visit; and, as he talked, very slowly and distinctly, I began to understand a little bit of what he said. . . .

All in all we visited the Deep South many times—enough to realize that the valley of separation still waits for a bridge, and to pray for a bridge where none exists so far. But in those early days we could only drive on in the bus, bewildered by a side of life which, as Europeans, we did not understand, and as Christians we could not approve.

To our surprise, we came to realize in traveling that America too is a country "on wheels." Some families stay home, but more families do not. It was not impossible for us to be entertained in a home in Mount Kisco, New York—and then, four months later, by the same people in their new home in Helena, Montana. Husbands are transferred. New opportunities open up, or old residential sections are condemned for new speed-

ways and super-highways. America spends more and more
money not to stay home. Besides—and here is one of the
first difficulties in the Americanization process of the refugee
—everything is standard: standard food, standard service,
standard brands, standard sizes—standard hotels. "Why is it,
Papa," the children would ask their father, "that in America
so many things are alike? Like a big basket of eggs, where
one egg is just like the other?"

(I remembered the question one memorable day when we
passed, on the super-highway, an overturned super-truck. No
one was hurt, but the entire freight, hundreds and hundreds
of super-fresh eggs, formed a great spreading yellow lake across
the road. "Look!" said Johannes. "A super-omelet!")

Small towns are standard, too, when each is made up of
Broad Street, Church Street, Main Street, and a business
section. Clapboards are standard. So are ho- and mo-tels.

During our first tours, I must say, we could not afford a
mo-, or even a second-best ho-; so, wherever we ended up for
the night, anyone we met in the lobby made us feel as though
we were in a gangster film. We had tiny rooms with the light
invariably just in the middle, and a mean little string to pull
that only Hedwig could ever seem to find. This she did by
standing in the center of the room waving her arms like a
conductor working up to his grand finale. Meanwhile, the rest
of us would be busy in the dark trying to stick our freshly
washed handkerchiefs on the one cracked mirror. After a few
years of this we could afford the larger hotels: the Knott Hotels, the Sheraton Hotels, the Statlers, the Hiltons, where
things went much better. We met up, too, with new standards—the standard hotel neighbor, typing vigorously through
the night on a not-noiseless typewriter; or the standard club
party that gets noticeably more cheerful from hour to hour
till, finally, its happy guests spend the rest of the night not-
finding their cars under your window; or the standard voice
at the desk saying, "Certainly, Madame," to your indignant
comments over the phone at 2:00 A.M.

Inevitably that soothing voice reminded me of a Tyrolean
mountain inn where I had once stayed with my husband.

Tony, the most valued member of their staff, was employed for the sole purpose of being fired—which he was, several times a day. Whenever a guest complained about anything at all—that his room was too cold or too hot; or the soup was salty or the food was not served on time—whatever the trouble, the proprietor of the hotel would call furiously, "Tony!" and in no time at all a very guilty-looking Tony appeared. The proprietor would scold him soundly, blame him for whatever had irritated the guest, and end in a loud crescendo, "You are FIRED!" Then Tony, broken-hearted, accepted, went back to his room and waited to be fired again. . . .

But all American methods are more streamlined. In America, even a proposal of marriage is streamlined. For instance: One night after a concert in Palm Beach I walked home alone. The balmy salt air and starry sky made me not too ready to go to bed, so for a few moments I sat down on a bench near the hotel. Suddenly, from behind me, a voice spoke out of the darkness, a youngish male voice:

"May I sit down too?"

I looked at the empty bench and said rather coldly, "There's room for at least five."

The voice sat down and started to talk. From my dress, he said, he thought I must be from Europe. Silence. He had liked Europe during the war. Very much. Silence. He would have liked to marry a European girl. But he was sent back too soon. Silence. Then the voice cleared its throat and said abruptly, "I want you to marry me. I assure you that you will not regret it. Down here we have a hurricane every other year—and I am in the roofing business!"

Of course we were more than once in that phenomenon of the New America, Hollywood—the center of every teen-ager's wishful thinking and the source of everything our land can offer in the line of cheap musicals, Westerns, and lurid love stories. Individuals in Hollywood seem pleasant and friendly enough—but for years we could find no basis for personal contact with them. We felt only an over-all superficiality in the parties that followed concerts; and, as with oil and water, we did not mix.

When J. B. Lippincott Company brought out *The Story of the Trapp Family Singers* we received a telephone call from Hollywood offering a large sum for the film rights. "You won't change the story, will you?" I happened to ask.

"Story?" came the answer. "We don't need the story—just the title. We make up our own story." We refused, and the offer was raised. We refused again. The Gloria Film, *Die Trapp Familie*, finally presented the screen version sympathetically, but in Europe.

So from one State to another we learned to know this new America with its concentration on exterior values and its bigger, better, identical "standards." Let no one think, however, that in all that time the Trapp Family remained—or even wished to remain—untouched by the Americanism of the country we had "discovered." Can I ever forget how proud I felt on that sunny morning when we all took Erika, Werner's fiancée just arrived from Austria, to breakfast in the Wellington drugstore? As we seated ourselves on the high stools along the counter, and met Mr. Schimmel's welcoming smile, I ordered first: "OJ, 2-3; draw; stack."

Erika looked at me blankly, and Lorli took over: "Large OJ, 51 and BLT down."

"Oh, no," I said, "Lorli, this is breakfast!"

"But, Mother, I'm hungry!"

"So am I," echoed Johannes. "GAC, 51, 81, too."

Father Wasner ordered a large OJ and a draw, while Erika, confused, said, "Coffee, please."

"Draw one," mumbled Johannes, then scribbled for a few moments on a slip of paper, and handed his future sister-in-law a neat little list which read:

Stack	Toast
Draw	Cup of Coffee
51	Hot Chocolate
81	Water
OJ	Orange Juice
TJ	Tomato Juice
2-3	Two eggs, boiled three minutes

BLT down   Bacon, lettuce and tomato sandwich on toast
GAC   Grilled American Cheese sandwich
Grade A   Milk
Burn   Malted Milk
Freeze   Frosted

"Make that a small OJ," I said suddenly, and Erika, taking courage, bravely gave her first order:

"Large OJ. Draw and stack. 81."

It was a wonderful breakfast. As we all left the drugstore together, Erika, Lorli and I exchanged triumphant glances of deep "standard" U.S.A. happiness. We had never felt so American.

8

The Real America

In America, California is not only Hollywood, and Florida is not always Palm Beach or Miami. We are so very different, one from another: Irish, Italian, Polish, French, Catholic, Protestant, Jew; but so often, in things that matter deeply, America shows its family closeness. That is why I can say so firmly that California—but later I will come back to the subject of Hollywood and the Florida resorts. This chapter really begins in Munroe, Michigan, on our first truly American Thanksgiving Day.

Early that morning a small white envelope pushed itself under the door of my "standard" hotel room. "Dear Baroness," the note read: "Our key is under the doormat. Just make yourself at home. We hope you will have a good time. M.M." and an address. The Trapp Family Singers, utter strangers in town, had been offered a home for Thanksgiving Day by a family who could not even be there to share it with us. We could hardly believe what we saw, as we stepped into "our" house in the residential section of Munroe. In the dining room a table was set for ten, with wine glasses and even two crystal decanters nearby.

On the table was a second note: "Dinner is almost ready in the kitchen." Led by Lorli and our own excellent sense of smell, we found a huge turkey already stuffed for roasting; a big bowl of salad on the table; and with it two mysterious pastries, our first pumpkin pie!

The whole heart-warming sight was so unexpected that it

really took our breath away. Rupert and Werner, with Lorli
and Rosmarie helpfully under foot, made a fire in the living-
room fireplace. Agathe and Hedwig directed operations in the
kitchen. My husband, peacefully smoking his pipe, looked
over the book-shelves, trying a volume here and there. Father
Wasner sat down at the piano and began quietly to improvise,
while, for the longest time, I stood at the window looking
out into nowhere and fighting down my tears of joy and
gratitude.

As we all came together around the table, Georg bade us
rise while he proposed the first toast: "To our absent hosts.
May God bless them in their undertakings a thousandfold."
Thus, without actually realizing it, we celebrated Thanksgiving Day in its proper spirit. We also took a big step forward
in the "discovery" of "our" country—for whose big heart all
the vast plains, towering trees, and high mountains are but
an appropriate setting. We were beginning to comprehend
something of the real America.

The real America is not neon-sign-language; it is a state
of mind. It is warm, spontaneous generosity—full measure,
pressed down and running over. For me it is summed up and
symbolized now by those early months in the United States.
Johannes was born in January, 1939, three weeks after our
first concert tour; and for that whole first year Professor Otto
Albrecht of the University of Pennsylvania was the pro-
tector of our sparsely furnished house in Germantown. We
learned right then and there that Quakers are rightly called
"Friends." Almost every morning brought a surprise on our
front porch: a warm blanket for a little crib, or chicken-all-
around for dinner.

While the baby was still only a few days old, the Carleton
Smiths arranged quiet for house and Mother by inviting all
lively younger Trapps to visit at their Do-re-mi Farm in
Connecticut. Rex Crawford, a friend of Otto's, came in one
afternoon with an armful of records; and, seeing that there
was no player in the house, made it his business to procure
one before the day was over. A year later the Crawfords took
one-year-old Johannes while we held to a concert schedule

in the South and West. Harry and Sophie Drinker casually
offered us a "large empty house" across the street from theirs.
Georg and I were told to take a vacation in a car that someone "didn't need."

A refugee is not just someone lacking in money and everything else. A refugee is vulnerable to the slightest touch: he
has lost his country, his friends, his earthly belongings. He
is a stranger, sick at heart. He is suspicious; he feels misunder-
stood. If people smile, he thinks they ridicule him; if they
look serious, he thinks they don't like him. He is a full-grown
tree in the dangerous process of being transplanted, with the
chance of possibly not being able to take root in the new soil.
As far as we are concerned, our dear Pennsylvania friends
took all these feelings away and made us secure; then, finally,
it was Craig Burt, of Stowe, who made us Vermonters at
heart.

I think I have mentioned in another book the gentleman
with the straw hat who "came calling" in our early Vermont
days, and how, at his request, we sang several days later for
Army men in a former C.C.C. camp not far from Cor Unum.
Afterwards, our "hat-man" thanked us heartily.

"Do come and see us," we urged.

"I might some day," he said. Not realizing that in Vermont
idiom this means, "tomorrow for sure," we made the mistake
of insisting—so it was weeks before he finally appeared. But
when he did, he helped us in the struggle with War Produc-
tion regulations and our own painful lack of funds as, with
the boys away in the Army, we worked to build up a tumble-
down farmhouse on a rocky hillside. Now, and to this very
day, he is our "Uncle Craig," a real old-timer, slow to talk,
ready to listen, keenly practical, with a sharp wit and a deep
love of the out-of-doors. At two family funerals he has walked
beside us; and in the gay "kitchen parties" of Cor Unum,
things are never more lively than when Uncle Craig regales
us with his stories. We have weathered many a storm with
his help, and we have learned to look at "the mountain" and
"the valley" through his eyes.

With Craig Burt we became part of Vermont; then Boston made us truly New Englanders. The year we received American citizenship, Frank Flanagan arranged for us to sing in the music-shell on the Charles River Esplanade in honor of the "I Am an American" Day. Even the boys, to our surprise, were flown in from Camp Hale to be present. We were truly touched when afterwards the Governor asked if there were anything he might do for us. Hesitating just a little, but with the confidence of an American-at-last, I finally said, "Mr. Governor, may I please sit next to the driver in a police car and blow the siren during the rush hour?" . . . At five that afternoon, a police car waited outside the hotel. We went loudly and gloriously through the city of Boston at top speed. . . .

As a matter of fact, it seems to me now that we were always touring one town or another at top speed. Time after time, our arriving bus would pull in, stop, and be greeted by the local committee, all bright and shining, with faces like freshly made beds.

"Welcome to X-bury, Mrs. Trapp," the chairman would say; then, after an exchange of greetings, "You aren't tired, are you?" No, of course we were not tired.

"That's fine," and the chairman would turn to her assembled group with: "All right, girls! There will be just time to show the Trapp Family the sights of X-bury!" Then, beaming at me: "You haven't seen X-bury yet, have you?"

No, we hadn't seen X-bury, though we might have seen A-bury, B-bury, C-bury and D-bury; so each time we departed again for a tour of a truly American Main Street, Broad Street, City Hall, Public Library, and High School. Local patriotism in the real America is not to be treated lightly. . . .

In the real America, Florida is not Palm Beach. After one of our concerts in a modest Florida resort town, the local manager, Mr. Green, came backstage and invited us to a "small Florida party." "One of my girls will drive you over," he said. Four girls promptly appeared: two were sixty-nine; one was seventy-eight; and one was eighty-two. Each, it seems, paid a lump sum per season as board and lodging in an at-

tractive cabin court for which Mr. Green was at one and the
same time business-manager, morale-builder, father, and
King Arthur. In the summer the whole business establish-
ment moved north to the State of Maine, and those who
wished could follow. In either place, his "Girls, I am proud
of you," brought glances of genuine admiration and grateful
love. Mr. Green certainly earned his living, but he also made
cloudlessly happy the ladies who had entrusted their well-
being into his hands. (The party was wonderful. I cannot
speak for the younger members of the Trapp Family, but we
"girls" all had a marvelous time!) It takes many people to
make up God's world.

In the real America California is not Hollywood. On our
second western tour, for instance, we were able to visit all
the early missions founded by the Franciscan Fathers who
came north, on foot, from Mexico. All seventeen missions
became old friends as we returned from time to time to these
age-old centers of Christian giving. Nor can we forget San
Juan Capistrano, where Werner's little Barbara, then aged
two, tried to play her favorite "This little piggy," with some
young Franciscan toes in sandals; and I shall always remember singing our old pilgrimage hymn to the Blessed Virgin,
Meerstern Ich Dich Grüsse, in Santa Barbara beside the
grave of a Franciscan Father who three months before had
been alive to tell us how he loved it. California is not Hollywood.

Perhaps I should say, too, that Hollywood is not always
Hollywood. When *The Story of the Trapp Family Singers*
first appeared, it was read by Mrs. Bob Hope's secretary.
After the last chapter about Cor Unum, she made up her
mind that Mrs. Hope and the children should plan their
vacation for the Green Mountains of Vermont. At the time
we had only the dimmest notion of who Bob Hope might be.
Casually we mentioned to some guests at Cor Unum that
Bob Hope's wife and children would be with us for August,
and the Green Mountains of Vermont suddenly echoed with
wild reactions. From Burlington to Montpelier and Morris-
ville, the news spread like wildfire: "Bob Hope's family is

going to stay with the Trapps." Queer stories went round,
and through the remaining weeks of waiting we became more
and more curious ourselves. Was it true that Mrs. Hope had
a complete outfit for every hour of the day? Would they in-
sist on eating from their own gold plates? Would she really
wash her face in goat's milk every morning because Bob
wanted her to keep that peaches-and-cream complexion?

Actually Dolores Hope did none of these things. On August first a modest station wagon arrived to deposit a mod-
erate amount of luggage, then the chauffeur drove off to
collect the arriving family at the Burlington airport. It was
love at first sight from the moment they arrived—Dolores,
Linda, Tony, Kelly, Nora, and Bella, the secretary. When
they left us at the end of the month, our Rosmarie went back
with them to Hollywood.

Not too long afterwards, en route from Hawaii to Los
Angeles, we all stopped there to help celebrate Bob Hope's
fiftieth birthday. Though every great name in Hollywood
was present, things were handled simply, and the house felt
like a home. In the receiving line I stood next to Dolores,
while the birthday child himself was far away at the children's
table, leading them in roars of laughter.

Perhaps it is just as well that he was no closer, in view of
what happened. In the line, Dolores handed a pleasant gentleman over to me with the words: "Maria, I want you to
meet Jack Benny."

"And what do *you* do?" I said, smiling pleasantly at Mr.
Benny. (Spencer Tracy was the only one I knew.)

"Why, Maria," Dolores laughed, "he's the nation's second-
best comedian!"

Wide-eyed, I thought that one over. Then I said, "Dolores,
who is the first one?"

Perhaps I should have gone to bed in disgrace, but a home
birthday party is a home birthday party. With shouts of
laughter around me, it seemed tactful instead just to join the
birthday child at the children's table. . . .

Our deepest appreciation of the real America, however,
came after the war, when a letter from an American general

with the Occupation Forces in Austria asked the Trapp Family to collect money and clothing for their former countrymen. People literally gave the coats off their backs for the Trapp Family Austrian Relief. There were days when our rolling bus had standing room only; days when we were all in the aisle because our seats were piled high with all the clothing, packages, food, and medicines that the people in forty-eight States had given us. As the bus traveled along between towns, we wrapped, tied, labeled in order to ship at the next town. With each stop, gifts poured in to us and the work was all to be done again.

Army chaplains in Austria—Father Nuwer in Vienna, with Father Saunders assisting in Salzburg—received the bundles for distribution. So many of them went directly to Salzburg that Father Saunders' orderly was reported to have said one morning pathetically, "Father, your mail has come. May I have a truck to get it?"

During summer sessions of our Music Camp, on the same spot where once we had sung for Uncle Craig's Army boys, campers threw themselves into the dirty, messy, tiresome details of sorting, packing and shipping. Mrs. Harper, a camper, came for a ten-day Sing Week in the summer of 1947—and stayed through the entire season as a volunteer worker. Some of her most solid help came from our dear friends, Marilyn Roode and the two Spaar sisters, not one of whom has ever had the gift of eyesight. Through it all, Martina and Agathe addressed labels, and Werner stood by to hoist finished bales onto the mail truck. For one of the hottest seasons in the history of Vermont the work went on, to the tune of a little theme song which was sung over and over again in the workshop:

> "Soprano, alto, tenor, bass—
> Our singing causes grief,
> But nothing equals packing for
> The Austrian Relief!"

Our old Archbishop in Salzburg had said slowly and pointedly, as he bade us farewell, "The fact that Father Wasner

goes with you now to America will one day be most beneficial
for this diocese." In that year, 1947, his prophetic words came
true; as with merriment, laughter, tears, blisters, and hard
work, over three hundred thousand pounds of supplies
were shipped by the Trapp Family Austrian Relief, leaving
our Music Camp for the country of Schubert, Mozart, and
Stille Nacht.

The "real America" made this possible—the open, spontaneous, unquestioning coast-to-coast generosity of the real
American—which I had first begun to sense and appreciate
through that quick note left for me years before in a Michigan hotel: "Dear Baroness: Our key is under the doormat. . . ."

9

Mañana

"Received offer for three months' South American tour. Want to go?" Freddy Schang's telegram reached us in Los Angeles early in 1950, during our spring tour of the West Coast.

Freddy never wastes words. Our answer, which we wired immediately, may perhaps have wasted two: "Yes—yes—yes." We were, nevertheless, a little sobered by the thought of a foreign tour. What all of us together had brought to America of Austrian traditions and Austrian music, what we had learned as Americans of American music and folk songs—we, the Trapp Family, were now once more to take abroad.

We wrote to Freddy immediately, asking: "When do we leave?"

Even then we had no real notion of what was ahead. We assumed the whole tour might be something like our previous experiences in Cuba—a matter of presenting a few concerts in a few well-organized towns, while well-organized friends would be always on hand to make sure that we said the right thing, in the right language, to the right person. In Cuba, thanks to our dear friends, Enriquetta and Ernesto Batista, concerts had gone smoothly in both Santiago and Havana, so that we loved remembering Cuba in many serene shades of green: grayish-green palm groves, dark laurels, yellowish aroma trees, lush sugarcane.

Johannes completely forgot, poor little boy, that in Havana he had picked the wrong kind of flower and awakened the next day with eyes and ears all swollen with blisters. I forgot, and I might have remembered, how dear to the heart of my son had been all the flowers, shells, snakes, and insects in Cuba. We all forgot—and for the good of our own stage presence, this should not have happened—the famous concert in Manzanillo, given on a warm evening in a barnlike "hall" with six doors opened wide into the street. Outside, all the vehicles of Manzanillo blew their horns at once, children on roller-skates shrieked and skated, street-criers put in an occasional descant, policemen whistled, and the Trapp Family sang on. During the sacred music a dog came leisurely up the aisle; and as Maria intoned the first solo bars of Mozart's *Ave Maria*, a cat crossed the stage. Somewhere in the wings a shower was running and could not be stopped, so the sound of water splashing down on a stone floor was heard through all numbers—even, appropriately enough, Father Wasner's arrangement of the Cuban folk song, *El Arroyo que Murmura*, which brought down the house with a loud response from audience, animals, and traffic, all at once.

But we forgot all this. Instead I searched my memory to recall Enriquetta's careful Spanish wording of my concert announcements, still wondering why my spoken Spanish had seemed to bring as much applause as our yodel numbers. I recalled, too—and in the bleak cold of a South American June the information was to prove absolutely useless—that five yards of wool in an Austrian dirndl can be very warm in Cuba. Agathe reminded a more-than-red-eared Johannes that in Spanish-speaking countries concerts sometimes begin after 10:00 P.M.—at which we all remembered the "Pro Arte" concert in Havana, sung on a hot night after a full day, and during which, as his mother sang *The Virgin's Lullaby*, Johannes' little head had sunk lower and lower on Martina's shoulder until, to the genuine joy of the audience, he was fast asleep.

All in all, we felt that South America could hold few surprises for us. There were only incidental question marks still to be settled. When would we leave? Where would we sing? When? Yet, curiously enough, Freddy Schang's answer, which reached us in the State of Washington, seemed to ignore these burning issues, merely telling us to start vaccinations against smallpox, yellow fever, and typhoid.

"When? Where? How many?" I wrote to Freddy. But his next letter was even less enlightening: he had, he informed us, specified to Señor Quesada, the South American manager, that Columbia Concerts would let us go only if an advance on our earnings, sufficient to insure our safe return to the U.S.A., were to be deposited in a New York bank. Our "question marks" temporarily dropped out of sight, as Father Wasner praised Freddy Schang for his prudence and foresight; while I, overcome by grave doubts, tried to think and talk of other things beside South America.

With arms aching and blooming from the typhoid shots, we went on to our concert in Denver. "It would be a shame," Hedwig said during the intermission, "to have gone all through this for nothing." Meanwhile, Maria, in the hotel bookstore, bought a South American handbook.

Silence from Freddy. Within the family, minor bets began to develop. One school of thought felt we would go down the Atlantic coast; six voices voted for the Pacific side, and Werner firmly said we would not go at all. On March twelfth came Agathe's birthday, and her seat in the bus was suddenly heaped high with birthday cake, dark glasses, sunburn cream, dramamine, and insect repellent. We reached Green Bay, Wisconsin, where a doctor from Tanganyika told us horror stories of the tropics. Solemnly we pledged never, NEV-ER (if) in South America to eat anything uncooked; and to drink no water. In Omaha, Nebraska, we gave a concert at the Convent of the Sacred Heart where the nuns lent us all their library literature on South America. I remember reading till two in the morning, then putting out my light with the firm impression that Santiago, Chile, looked like Innsbruck and that Guatemala seemed to have the most lovable Indians. . . .

Next, in Cincinnati, Ohio, came the famous April Fool's Day: "Mother, quick, Mr. Quesada is on the phone from Buenos Aires!" A masculine voice informed me, in broken English, that he was impatient to make my acquaintance—

and that while in South America I should drink no water, only champagne. I recognized Werner. In Bowling Green, Kentucky, a second medical check. As far as the doctors were concerned, we were ready to go. But otherwise—silence.

Finally, in Springfield, Illinois, came a letter from Columbia Concerts saying noncommittally that if we left at all, it would be on Easter Sunday, April ninth, at 9:00 A.M. By April fourth we had reached Columbus, Ohio, and there was still no word, so I decided to fly to New York. There my worst suspicions were all confirmed: no money; no visas; no tickets.

The family were to arrive by bus the next day—Holy Saturday. Throughout Good Friday, April seventh, I must have called Freddy Schang every hour on the hour asking anxiously for news, while a patient voice told me there was none. Then I tried getting used to the idea that perhaps this was not the Will of God. After all, Good Friday is the day for a special sacrifice, so I prepared to meet the family's disappointment with a radiant smile. . . .

And then . . . on Holy Saturday morning the impossible happened. Freddy called to say that he had round-trip plane tickets for us—Quesada had wired the advance. The family appeared, heard the words "really going," and plunged into frantic last-minute shopping. Long-distance telephone reached Cor Unum, where Erika hastily left for New York to wave goodbye. With Barbara, she would go on to visit her parents in Salzburg.

By nightfall we were all together, in time to share our "Pascal lamb"—a mild little raisin-eyed creature located by Lorli in a bakery across from the Wellington. . . .

In the dark hours of the early morning, the Gradual of the Easter Mass seemed strangely fitting—"Haec dies, quam fecit Dominus"—as did two little words of the Sequence: "Praecedet vos—He shall go before you." Quickly each one of us crowded last-minute things into her "mops," while Father Wasner worked to persuade me, and I was less than persuadable, that the dictaphone, Dormiphone, and "DC-3" mu-u-st stay at home. Once more the good old bus took us out of

New York to the airport, where we found Freddy Schang
himself. Then suddenly the plane was called. There were
quick, painful goodbyes, the roar of motors as strong wheels
took us down the runway and, finally, the air—with the fields
faintly green below us and a high wind blowing us along.

In the plane Hester handed me an envelope from Señor
Quesada. At last, our South American itinerary. I had become accustomed to Columbia Concerts' meticulous listing
of dates, towns, halls, hours, hotels, and managers. Sr. Quesada's memo was, I must say, new and different:

April 11.   Puerto Rico. Second concert only if first suc-
             cessful.
April 14.   Possible concert in Mayagüez. Answer pend-
             ing.
April 15.   Possible concert in San Germán. Answer
             pending. If San Germán does not take place,
             try concert at Collegio del Sacrado Corazón.
April 15.   Leave for Caracas. Exact date and hour of
             this concert not specified. Ask at airport on
             arrival.
April 17.   Leave Caracas for Aruba. Hour of flight later.
             Two (?) concerts.
April 19.   Curaçao. Concert evening.
April 20.   Caracas. Possible third concert.
April 21.   Leave Caracas for Port of Spain. Possible
             concert. Details later.
April 22.   Arrive Belém. Concert maybe.

And so on, and so on, through to Rio de Janeiro. Everything was flexible, possible, elastic, uncertain, and *mas o
menos*. Pinned to the list of Señor Quesada's irregularities
was a little note from Freddy Schang:

"Courage. You are entering the Country of *Mañana*."

Suddenly Father Wasner announced that one suitcase, containing all the music we would need for the next three
months, had been left behind in New York . . .

Memories of our stay in Puerto Rico are punctuated by Hester's daily attempts to reach New York by phone:

"No, the brown suitcase . . . *brown* . . . the *BROWN* suitcase is missing!"

(The brown suitcase, once launched, followed us through the entire tour, and finally caught up in Texas as we headed for home. By that time Father Wasner had written out most of the music again, and we had learned a new attitude: "Why worry? . . . *mañana!*")

We were told that success in South America would depend on Puerto Rico, and that Puerto Rico would depend on San Juan, so we went to the San Juan "Pro Arte" concert with all the sensations accompanying a "first" in Town Hall or the Salle Plateau in Montreal.

We seemed to make it. Even after our last encore, the Brahms *Lullaby*, the curtain rose and rose again, while people stood crowded in front of the stage applauding and whistling. Afterwards they came running to the wings, volubly overflowing in Spanish, English, or sign language; and one noble gentleman—Latin enthusiasm is wonderfully spontaneous—weepingly embraced me, with the fervent comment: "You biggest mother in world!"

So we were a success, and the next day our manager telephoned the news over the mountain to Ponce. Ponce advertised us all day through the city by taxi-loudspeaker; and when "biggest mother" and family arrived that evening, the hall was filled to capacity, including people who had heard us before in Chicago, Boston, and New Orleans. The next morning, at the Convent of the Sacred Heart, we even met some Sisters of St. Joseph from that fine old Spanish town of Brooklyn. It was a time for meeting old friends, but Johannes, with the tenacity of a real scientist, spent that morning collecting tropical flowers, and pressing them in an old schoolbook by the simple means, frequently repeated, of sitting down suddenly and hard.

"Mother," he inquired thoughtfully as we walked through the streets of Ponce together, "how much do you weigh?"

"One hundred and sixty pounds," I answered; thankful

that Rupert's medical practice held him at that moment in faraway Rhode Island.

"Wow!" Johannes whistled. "Fifty pounds more than I!" I felt touched, elderly, and ready to accept when, a few minutes later, my young escort asked whether I might not feel tired and like to rest a moment. We sat down together on a stone bench. Only when Johannes, quick as a monkey, slid his bulging book under me, did I get the point! . . .

I can still see myself the next morning sitting on one of our large suitcases at the airport, making angry little notes in my diary, such as: "We are all tired and cranky. The loudspeaker says our plane is late. Instead of 5:00 A.M., we will now leave at 6:00 A.M." We finally left, at 8:15, while I wrote furiously: "Was it for this that we got up at 3:30?"

As the plane rose into the sky, I looked around me. I could see Hedwig already asleep in her seat. Maria was winding wool, Martina was writing a letter, and across the aisle Lorli was making friends with a little Puerto Rican baby. The others were somewhere behind me. The sun was bright, and beyond the wings of the plane white clouds sailed by like huge prehistoric animals. Below us were blue depths and white mist. Behind us Puerto Rico looked briefly like an emerald fading into blue velvet. Then our plane banked, turned, rose, and rose again as we headed for Venezuela.

10

Il Coro Trapp: A Family on Wings

Everything is different under the Southern Cross. Keys are put in the locks upside down. To call someone to you, you wave him away. A tropical sun shoots up without warning from below the horizon and plunges suddenly down at night, pulling a heavy blanket of darkness over its head. Stars hang in the sky like Christmas tree decorations—and a "family on wheels" becomes a "family on wings," as our twenty thousand dollars in flight tickets and thirty thousand miles in the air can more than prove.

My memory-pictures of South America are like a kaleidoscope. The same names and places come back to me over and over again, always in a different connection. As concert artists, we had one set of impressions; as tourists and travelers, another. I must apologize because they refuse to arrange themselves in any kind of chronological order. I could write ten books about South America.

But to come down to earth. . . .

We landed in Venezuela under a forbidding-looking wall of red rock towering straight up out of the sea. Somewhere up above us was Caracas.

"Mother, look!" cried Johannes, as three dare-devil taxis bringing us up from the airport stopped at a red light. "That sign says we sang here yesterday!"

With unbelieving eyes we all read the huge "three-sheet," listing concerts to be given in Caracas by "Il Coro Trapp"—and one of them unmistakably the day before.

"A printer's mistake," said Sr. Quesada, peering over Johannes' shoulder. Sr. Quesada (Junior, only—his father was located in Havana) had proved to be *muy simpático*, with gentle, faintly reproachful English-setter eyes and a bouquet of eighty roses for each of us!

"Why wasn't the printer's mistake corrected?" we asked. His mild shrug implied: "What a typically Northern question!"

Hedwig was the first to recover. "Who ever called this the country of *mañana?*" she inquired, but I was already won, so taken in by the compelling three-sheet that I almost asked Father Wasner if our press reviews had been favorable that morning.

It was always like that in South America. Sometimes, it is true, we were reminded of our hundreds of Community Concerts back home, especially when local committees met us at the airport with just time to show us the sights of São X—— or San Z——; but more often than not, we were reminded of nothing that had ever happened to any of us before. For our "second" concert in Caracas, the hall was half empty; for the third it was sold out; and, as we were taking our departure for the Dutch West Indies, Sr. Quesada surprised us with the announcement that he had arranged a fourth. We would have to come back again. I must say that I greeted the news somewhat coldly, as our three taxis were just then shooting down a narrow, steep highway to the water, sliding around hairpin turns and threatening momentarily to plunge off into the abyss. When we finally got out of the car, my knees could have been stirred with a spoon. I had never been so frightened, not even on my one experience with a roller-coaster at Rye Beach. The last thing I hoped to do was come back. . . .

But we did. It seems to me now that we sang for everyone in South America. We gave concerts for children and concerts for seminarians. We had radio spots and full-length radio programs. At one point we were sponsored by a hosiery manufacturer who presented each of us with five pairs of nylons. We sang in churches, concert halls, and convents—or in the open air. We nearly collapsed from the heat in Caracas

and nearly froze in Buenos Aires, but we kept on singing; and
never, never, did we at any point know what was coming next.
The only thing we got used to was not getting used to things.

The experience of Caracas was constantly repeated. We
would be told backstage during an intermission, for instance,
to prepare immediately for six more concerts; and the following week would find us traveling rapidly back and forth
between, say, São Paulo, Curitiba, Ponta Grossa, Pôrto Al-
legre, and São Leopoldo. On the other hand, if we put a
direct question, such as: "How many concerts do we give
here?"—the answer might be:

"One. More if you fill the hall."

"And if we do *not* fill the hall?" Martina misguidedly once
asked that.

"Then" (pleasant voice and friendly nod) "you will simply
return home."

Actually the "gateway" concert—the most important one
for our future reputation as concert artists—was certainly the
one in Buenos Aires. Mr. Schraml, the local manager, told
us, in the dripping rain at the airport, that Buenos Aires'
Teatro Colón is second in importance only to La Scala in
Milan. We felt very serious when a cousin of my husband's,
Prince Auersberg, an *émigré* to Argentina and a member of
the large German-speaking colony in Buenos Aires, drove over
for a brief visit with us, expressing controlled concern as to
whether the Teatro Colón might not be above our ability.
A letter from Señor Quesada in Havana waited us at the
hotel, answering in a friendly way my written reports of our
success so far, but adding: "Let's wait for Buenos Aires. That
will decide how good you really are."

Full of misgivings, we began intensive rehearsals. There is
a law in Argentina that concert programs such as ours must
include one piece by an Argentinian composer, and we had
none. Mr. Schraml quickly decided on Gustavino's *Pueblito
Mi Pueblo*, which was delivered to us by the composer in
person. Within twenty-four hours Father Wasner had made a
choral setting, and we had learned the—Spanish!—words by

heart. We decided also to practice old familiar German songs, such as *In einem Kühlen Grunde*.

A visit to the Teatro itself did not help us at all. It seats well over three thousand people, and beside it the Vienna Opera House would be as nothing. The fourth gallery is dizzily high and far away from the stage. Besides, though the Church calendar told us it was the week before Pentecost, in Argentina that meant late fall. Our hotel was large, cold, gloomy, sad-colored, disheartening; and a cold rain knocked at the windows. For our last tense rehearsal, we sat with numb feet and stiff fingers, wrapped in blankets and huddled together around one tiny electric heater. Finally, in the cold pouring rain, we drove off to the Teatro Colón, feeling as though we were heading for a musical guillotine.

Two hours later "Il Coro Trapp" had discovered that Argentina's freezing temperatures can be dispelled by the warmth of an audience. A great cloud of love and enthusiasm came from the hall to the stage, surrounding us and lifting us off our feet. There were seven encores and seven curtain calls. People gathered below the stage clapping, shouting, and refusing to go home. *Pueblito Mi Pueblo* was a great success; and so, it appears, was our Spanish. So was our sacred music, and so were the Austrian and American folk songs.

At last we could breathe again. We were so happy—and, after having been kissed and embraced by the Schramls and Auersbergs, we embraced and kissed one another. Sr. Quesada's second son, the one taking care of Argentina and the west coast, congratulated us warmly on this true success and said, "Now South America is open for 'Il Coro Trapp.'" After that concert, we had all the sensations of a young pilot receiving his first wings. When, in the early morning hours, we finally returned home, even the hotel seemed to have warmed up just a little.

There was a second concert, then a third in the Teatro Colón, followed by programs in Santa Fé and Rosario—where, by way of contrast and surely to keep us humble, we made more mistakes than ever in our lives before. Even Johannes got stuck on the recorder, and Father Wasner was pale with frustration. . . .

Other concerts here and there will always stand out as distinct memories, even though today, nearly nine years later, I am a little confused as to just which came when. I remember Aruba as a flat, sandy little island, covered with cactus and heavy with oil interests, where the flowers presented to us had been flown in the night before from Colombia and Holland. Recife was distinguished by its "local committee" —a lone, be-monocled gentleman who met us at the airport with a face "as unlive as a shop window at three o'clock in the morning" (Lorli). Through his cool appraising glance, the monocle sparkled with undisguised disapproval. "Hoddya-dew," he said in an antiseptic voice—and stalked away, leaving us to reach the town by ourselves. (Dear "girls" of X-bury, how I longed for you!) After the concert, he reappeared backstage, adjusted the monocle, and remarked, "Quite nice." Then he made his way out through the whistling, shouting, stamping audience, and disappeared.

Bahía was memorable because of a particularly elaborate Brazilian dinner after which Johannes observed: "The difference between mealtime for a boa constrictor and mealtime for 'Il Coro Trapp' is that the boa constrictor never has to give a concert right afterwards!"

Our most uncertain concert was probably in Lima, Peru, though by that time we were really accustomed to the unexpected. It was dark when we arrived, and the local manager, a timid little man, came to the airport to ask us in all seriousness whether we might not prefer to stay in the plane and continue right on. There would be no concert in Lima, he said, because an Italian opera company was in town, and he did not dare risk the competition. We were disappointed, but Lima is the city of Santa Rosa, Rosmarie's patron saint, so, to the little man's dismay, all our luggage came out of the plane, as a sign of our firm decision to spend the night at least. . . .

And we did give a concert! Old friends of the family, the Gildemeisters, neighbors of former days in Austria, helped us find a hall, rent it, and fill it—all within the space of twenty-four hours. Until the curtains actually opened, we did not know whether there would be anyone in the hall. But why worry? By then we were seasoned old-timers in South America. We left Peru slightly wilted but happy.

Santiago de Chile is certainly worthy of mention. In the Teatro Municipal, when we arrived for our evening concert, a large crowd was pouring out of all the doors. Claudio Arrau had just finished giving an afternoon concert in his native land—to a full house. No one—no one normal, that is—buys two tickets to two concerts on the same day; so, half an hour later, when the curtains finally parted for "Il Coro Trapp," we could only urge our audience to fill in the first three rows! It was not one of our best concerts.

Memories of Rio are particularly vivid. I know that Rio for Hedwig meant the breath-taking air view of a city nestling close under its towering Sugar Loaf, with the sea cutting deep fjord-like bays, like the fingers of a hand, into the mountainous coast. For Agathe, who suffers from the heat, it meant fifty thousand people surf-bathing at once. To Lorli, Rio meant the highlight of the whole trip—and one which had nothing to do with music—a real flood, between our first and second concerts; a cloudburst that flooded streets, washed away houses, and marooned us in a bus for two hours in the pitch dark. To Johannes Rio meant the capture backstage of a prize treasure, which he proudly exhibited to us in a shoe-box—the largest spider we had ever seen, with eight legs each as big as my little finger.

"Mother, just feel the lovely little fur he has!" said my son —and failed to appreciate why Mother gymnastically put six yards and two large concert suitcases between herself and the sweet exhibit.

Rio to Father Wasner meant Doña María Emilia, Sr. Quesada's Brazilian representative, a tiny lady with a friendly face, who kept us waiting for hours at the airport, feeling like animals in a zoo, then rushed us forever afterwards from one concert to the next.

For me, however, as I look back on it, Rio means just one

thing: *Saudade. Saudade,* ("Nostalgia") is a Brazilian folk song which Doña María Emilia produced for us just before the second Rio concert. It comes from a part of Brazil where there are such long droughts, sometimes for two years or more, that entire villages and towns have to travel north with families and herds into the Amazon Valley. The nostalgia of a people in exile has produced many beautiful songs, but this one we took immediately to our hearts:

"Não ha ò gente ò não luar come este de sertão—There is no moon but the moon out in the field." The melody is grave and haunting, filled with longing and patient, hopeful waiting. From Rio on, the song was included in our repertoire. *Saudade—Heimweh*—the longing-for-home. For the last South American concert of "Il Coro Trapp," with faces already turned towards the United States, we sang it as an encore, and with mixed feelings; for by then our own *saudade* reached out to bear on and include things past as well as things ahead.

11

Snakes, Ants, and Missionaries

Once as a student I took a course in the History of Art. Most of all I remember a piece of Greek sculpture called the Laocoön: a father and sons, all of them wrapped up in boa constrictors and not liking it. I absolutely did not blame them for that, and I never quite managed to forget them, especially after South America, where I had to remember them.

Not everyone, in his day-to-day living, has the blood-curdling opportunity to encounter, all of a sudden, ten feet of snake hanging from a tree and swaying gently in the warm afternoon breeze. (I did—in the jungle, and later I shall come back to that.) Not everyone is permitted, as we were in São Paulo, to visit a world-famous snake institute like the Butantan. Johannes was in his seventh heaven peering at poisonous serpents, spiders and scorpions; and at the end of the visit I had to take, with averted eyes, an off-center photograph of a small boy wrapped proudly in twenty feet of python.

Even that was not the end. The worst moment came in São Leopoldo, when I heard: "Mother, there's a Jesuit Father here who has *tamed* poisonous snakes! Mother . . ."

"No," I thought, "never in my life!" Johannes' collection already included forty-two boxes of shells, stones, and insects; a large map of Brazil; a blow-tube and four poison darts; a head-hunter club; and a real Indian bow. All we needed now . . . but just the same I melted and let myself be taken to visit the "snake-Father."

My worst premonitions were confirmed when my eleven-year-old son and I were ushered into a big empty room that looked like a biology laboratory. Suddenly a warning voice spoke somewhere behind us: "Move quietly, please. One of my poisonous snakes has escaped, and I want to catch it."

We didn't move quietly. We didn't move at all. We stood rooted to the spot. With all my heart I wanted the search to be successful, and we waited in absolute silence for an infinite time, while the Jesuit Father went down on his knees, peering under big chests, until, with coaxing sounds and a bowl of milk, he persuaded his darling to return.

Radiant envy appeared on Johannes' face . . . and, at that point, I definitely turned towards the door. "Come, Johannes," I said, "I am sure we have a rehearsal." Whether or not such a rehearsal had been planned before, it would be now; and I escorted my protesting son out of the room. Behind us, the Jesuit Father remained on his knees in the big laboratory, tenderly handling his snakes—Paradise fashion, before the Fall.

This chapter, however, is really about the jungle and Father Kraeutler, who introduced us to it. Father Kraeutler is a missionary of the Society of the Most Precious Blood who once, on a fund-raising visit to the United States, had come to visit us in Stowe with gruesome stories about savage Indians in the Amazon Valley. Now, suddenly, he turned up at the airport in Belém, just as we were arriving.

There are two ways of leaving a plane: (a) expecting someone to meet you; (b) not expecting someone to meet you. At Belém we were following Plan B, when the sound of Tyrolean dialect hit our ears: *Familie Trapp, herzlich willkommen in Brazilien!*—and there was Father Kraeutler, smiling all over. What a surprise!

"I didn't know, Father, that you were stationed in Belém," said Father Wasner. "I thought you were in the upper Amazon with the—which Indians is it?"

"Xingu," answered Father Kraeutler. (It sounded like "Sching-goo.") "No, I am not stationed in Belém at all. I am here to get supplies of food and medicines for my Indians, and it took me four days of traveling on a river boat to come down."

Standing on the airfield, even in the warm darkness, we were suddenly aware, somewhere out beyond us, of the presence of the jungle, beautiful and terrible, pressing in upon the town. "It does exactly that," Father Kraeutler told us the next day after Holy Mass in the great ghostlike cathedral of Belém. "The underbrush is beginning to push right up to the last back yards of the city and the jungle is moving in." We looked at one another.

It was Agathe, usually so quiet, who voiced everyone's secret thought. "Father," she asked hopefully, "couldn't *we* visit the jungle?"

So that started it. Immediately after lunch, when most people in the tropics are having a siesta, the Trapp Family drove through the silent streets of Belém and out along the narrow dirt roads to a point where cars had to be left. After that we followed Father Kraeutler single file down a narrow footpath that drew us deeper and deeper into a green wilderness where no trace of blue sky could be seen. There were pale green palms and deep green palms. There were trees whose whole trunk was covered with thorns. There were huge green domes and multitudes of orchids. There were locust trees with their quaint fruit called St. John's Bread. There were trees which, when their bark is bruised, shed drops of blood-red tears.

It was extremely warm and damp. Maria whispered that her shoes were growing moldy, and Lorli prophesied that we might all look like Roquefort cheese before the afternoon was over. We went on, watched over by monkeys and parrots and many small hidden eyes. "Yet in the midst of all this life," Father Kraeutler remarked, "one can still manage to starve to death. The trees are too tall, the trunks are too thorny. Animals are either too shy or too sly to be caught by the white man. Even with so many things growing, men have died here for want of food."

Just then, with a few soprano and alto gasps of alarm, we came to the snake in the tree and passed by more than cautiously. Father continued, "Snakes are not the real danger of the jungle." He pointed suddenly, and our eyes, following the direction of his finger, watched, fascinated, a long column of small, determined ants, swarming up the base of a tree. "If Brazil does not destroy those little creatures, they will destroy Brazil. There's also a fire ant whose bite hurts terribly, and a water ant, that can make a burn one or two inches deep. There are termites. There are even some that can finish off cattle, horses, and whole towns."

As he finished speaking, we came suddenly to a little clearing with the ruins of a stone building. Its roof had long since gone; its chimneys were cracked and sagging; its walls, still standing, were heavily overgrown with the tough, thick roots of a choking fig tree. We stopped. After quite a long silence, Father Kraeutler said, "This is an old Carmelite church and convent. Years ago it was a mission. Somehow it always seems to me the symbol of my life's work. I have several different mission stations throughout the jungle, but as soon as I leave one for another, the Indians relapse into their former heathen practices. It's like the choking fig tree, and each time, all over again, there is the new clearing to be made in the wilderness." The lines in his face went suddenly deeper.

No one said a word. Were it not for our concert engagements and Sr. Quesada's tickets, we would all gladly have stayed on with Father and the Xingu Indians. Johannes, with a child's fine instinct, suddenly locked both arms around the missionary's waist. "Father—" and his big blue eyes looked pleadingly up into the drawn face—"Father, I will tell everyone about your mission."

"Thank you," said Father Kraeutler.

Two minutes later he was laughing and joking with us, making us all sit down on the ruined walls of the old convent while he told us stories of the headhunters. When the moment came, we could hardly bear to part from this man who two days later would go back up the river, never knowing— as indeed the gallant group of American missionaries murdered in 1956 by the Auca Indians could not have known —whether he would return alive. . . .

We visited many missions and met many missionaries in South America: "Los Padres Alemanes," The Society of the Divine Word, on Pentecost Sunday in Buenos Aires; Carmelites in Chile on the Feast of Corpus Christi; in São Leopoldo, Father Hofer, a Jesuit from Switzerland; American Redemptorists in Belém. One night after the Ponta Grossa concert we were suddenly addressed backstage in English by four young men from the United States—Mormon missionaries from Utah who had hoped for time to visit with us. The only possible suggestion, since we were busy for the evening, was "Why don't you come tomorrow to our Mass at six-thirty and afterwards we can have breakfast together."

With true missionary zeal they were present at the appointed time. At breakfast afterwards the leader of the group promptly presented me with a copy of *The Book of Mormon*, personally inscribed "To Mrs. Maria Trapp." So it happened that, when the book was accidentally left behind on a bench of the waiting room at the airport, a loudspeaker broadcast over the entire field, "Mrs. Trapp, your *Book of Mormon* has been found. . . ."

We also sang in a Lutheran girls' school in Hamburgo Velho and for a Lutheran Theological College in São Leopoldo. It was really wonderful to sing for these serious young men who asked for a program of sacred music; and when, at the very end, we invited them to join with us, a hundred strong voices rose together in a Bach chorale.

In Rio we visited the Benedictine monastery, São Bento, where we had a long talk with some of the German monks. There was so much to say and think and feel about the missions as we had seen them in South America; and I realized the "choking-fig" Indians, or those who had never heard the Gospel preached, did not disturb me nearly so much as empty indifference or ignorance in some of the souls who had. I still cannot forget the case of Juan in Argentina, a "good boy" whose religious instruction had been so scant that he was bewildered by Holy Mass and—we later learned to our horror —made his First Communion that day with us, not knowing what he did. Why does this incident come together in my mind with the trees of the blood-red tears? Or why do I associate such spiritual emptiness with broken walls in a green jungle and the sound of Father Kraeutler's voice saying, "In the midst of all this life, one can still manage to starve to death"?

I was still turning these questions over in my mind on the morning of the day we were to leave São Leopoldo, when Father Hofer came in with a message from the Rector of the Seminary, asking if I would address the seminarians before leaving. "On what?" I asked.

"Anything that is close to your heart," Father Hofer answered. . . . So it happened that I was privileged to meet, in the largest Brazilian seminary, young seminarians from twenty different dioceses, and I talked less to them about the language of Scripture than about a simple, basic, elementary language that can reach all peoples where no words are spoken—the language of kindness.

I told them about Mr. Fischer, a friend we had made in Curaçao. He had met us at the plane radiating kindness and charity. As a professional photographer, he had stayed up all night—and more of this later—developing some important pictures for us. He had driven us at breakneck speed to catch a plane for Caracas, stopping even at that urgent moment to take on a lonesome hitchhiker and give directions to a fat little out-of-town sailor. I can still see Mr. Fischer refusing an invitation to the beach with us and saying mournfully in Austrian dialect:

"Wanni nur net so viel Ueberfluss an Zeitmangel haett! —If only I didn't have so much surplus lack of time!"

I asked the seminarians to be apostles of the heart and the heart's language. And then I went on talking, to tell them how we had all felt about Juan and the head-hunters, and Father Kraeutler, and I put the language of kindness beside the language of music.

12

Flights, Bites, and Stings

Three separate flights—and for quite different reasons—stand out as memorable in all our miles of airborne travel. If the family were asked, for instance, which trip they enjoyed the most, I am sure they would answer in chorus (soprano, alto, tenor, bass): "Trinidad to Belém!" From the very beginning of the flight we were fascinated by the gentleman across the aisle. We could not make out his nationality, and we speculated among ourselves in stage whispers. Suddenly, in faultless German, the gentleman introduced himself: Mr. Balluder, American-born, German-educated, and Vice President of Pan American Airways.

At this point the voice of the captain came over the loudspeaker announcing that we were approaching Cayenne in French Guiana and that immediately afterwards we would cross over Devil's Island. "Oh," said Lorli, almost with tears of disappointment, "and here we are, seven thousand feet high. We won't see a thing!"

Mr. Balluder overheard her. Somewhere, it seems, he had been to one of our concerts. He called the captain. . . . In a few moments we felt the plane dip, turn, and go down; then, far below us, but very clearly, we saw the three islands: Ile Saint Joseph, Ile Royal, and—most memorable of all—the Ile du Diable. For me at that moment all human misery, all the stings of injustice we human beings seem so readily to inflict on one another, were caught and held and symbolized by that tiny bleak speck in the water—Devil's Island, where for so long Alfred Dreyfus, a French Army officer falsely accused of treason, was kept prisoner, with sharks and sun and pestilence for company.

The plane rose again. The sun went down, and we slept a little. Then, with a sickening thud, we dropped three hundred feet, and every light in the plane went out. "Here we go," I thought, and—of all things—"To think that brown suitcase never made it!" But the plane righted itself. Lights went on; the door of the cabin opened; and Jupiter, the Neptune of the air, made a regal entrance with his court. His Majesty solemnly announced to a goggle-eyed Johannes that the bump we had just felt came from crossing the Equator, and he handed each newcomer to his kingdom a certificate. (My son still has his, though some half-unsuccessful plant-pressing in Chile did permanent things to it.)

Far below in the distance, lights appeared, the lights of Belém. "Fasten your seat-belts," said the stewardess. It was a definite thrill to realize that for the first time we were really south of the Equator and in the southern hemisphere. Proudly we clutched our diplomas and prepared to leave the plane. Our flight from Trinidad to Belém was over.

That was the family's favorite. *My* favorite flight took us from Ecuador to Cali, Colombia. As we waited in the airport, I stood checking our route on a huge wall map. Chimborazo— the name leaped out at me, a familiar name and I could not remember why. Then it all came back to me with a vision of a little Austrian girl in a school pinafore—myself—tearfully writing one hundred times: "The Chimborazo is the highest peak in Ecuador." I was still thinking of her as the plane was called and we climbed aboard. When the captain passed my seat, I absolutely had to ask him, "Do we go anywhere near the Chimborazo?"

"No, *ma'am!*" he answered, "that *would* be out of the way." Silence, while I struggled with tears of disappointment. Then I could not stand it, rose from my seat over Father Wasner's prudent protests, and hammered on the door reading, "No Admittance."

"Captain"—I burst pleadingly into the cockpit—"how far out of the way would it be?"

"All of forty miles, ma'am."

"But, Captain, what is forty miles for an airplane? Nothing at all!"

"Yeh, but forty miles one way! If you want to reach Bogotá today, you have to make connections in Cali. We're late already."

Silence, then suddenly I saw my advantage. "Captain," I begged, "if we are late already, a few more minutes won't make much difference. Take your telephone here," and I handed him the instrument, "call Cali and tell them you are on the way with ten passengers for Bogotá."

Silence. "Even if I did that," said the captain, weakening, "you'd never see the Chimborazo. There's a photographer from Cali been coming with me for two years almost once a week, and we haven't got it yet. Always hidden in the clouds."

"Can't we try, Mother?" Johannes was at my elbow. I had not seen him follow me into the cockpit. His expression of deep disappointment seemed to do the trick. Long silence.

"O.K.," said the young captain. He telephoned Cali, offered us the co-pilot's seat, swerved the plane sharply to the right, and started to climb. Up we went—up and up and up—ten thousand, fifteen thousand, eighteen thousand feet. With gestures, the captain produced oxygen tubes and showed us how to adjust them. Then all at once we seemed to head straight for a curtain of dense white clouds.

"That's it," yelled the pilot over the roar of the motors. "That's where your Chimborazo *would* be if you could see it!"

Then came the unbelievable. At that moment, clouds were suddenly slashed by an invisible sword. The heavy white curtains were literally drawn to both sides as for a giant opera; and in the opening a perfect pyramid of brilliant white ice stood out suddenly against a background of deep intense blue.

"The Chimborazo!" we shouted with one voice, and our captain added vehemently:

"Wow!"

Closer and closer he brought the plane, banked, and cir-

cled twice in a closely drawn loop, while we gazed fascinated into the deep green crevasses. Then, in a second, while
we still held our breath, the curtain of clouds closed in once
more, and the nose of the plane headed out towards our
waiting connection in Cali.

"Thank you, Captain!" I said with a deep sigh of gratitude.

"Wasn't that something!" The young pilot seemed to be
quite enthusiastic himself.

"Does everything always turn out so well for you?" I asked.
He was silent for a minute.

"Well, ma'am," he said suddenly, "I hope so. There's a
girl in Lima I aim to persuade to marry me. . . ."

We parted friends in Cali—and were relieved a few weeks
later to have a card sent by our captain—from Lima. He
sounded . . . happy.

We left Rio by plane, rising slowly, flying close over the
Corcovado. The Corcovado is a high mountain at the entrance to the harbor. On top of it stands the great familiar
figure of Christ, blessing the world with outstretched hands.
The wide gesture, especially when seen from so near, seems
more than ever to radiate power and kingship and compassion, reaching out over Rio, past the Chimborazo, beyond
every misery of Devil's Island, to invite all human weakness
and all human hope. Far below, town, harbor, and townsmen
were motionless for a moment like painted toys, then they
disappeared behind us over the blue rim of the distance. . . .

But South America was not all smooth flying. Traveling
life, first of all, was much more tiring than back home, where
the bus could roll easily from one town to the next. Varied
new impressions and emotions told on us, with strange foods,
strange customs, strange flowers, and even different stars at
night. We hopped breathlessly from one spot to the next—
anxious to go on, anxious to linger—until it all reminded me of
times at home when our bus would shoot through the Yosem-
ite Valley or the Painted Desert, then deposit us for three
long days between concerts in, say, Kokomo, Indiana.

Besides, in Argentina it was cold and rainy; in Ecuador, it was hot and damp. Everywhere, a certain hush came down as people talked about their government. Sometimes, in that spring of 1950, we were reminded of our own last days in Hitler-invaded Austria.

We had to get used to the fact that the big cities of South America are really international melting-pots, and here and there we found ourselves at a stiff formal diplomatic reception where conversation had a boneless quality that was all form, no content, with much fluent talk going on and on, spinning effortless words out of nothing. "Sometimes," Maria remarked after one of those parties, "I wonder if these people talk because they think sound is easier to manage than silence."

The melting-pot situation produced a very embarrassing incident in Brazil where one evening, as we were sitting at a big round table in the hotel dining room, we were approached by a quite ordinary-looking gentleman in a blue business suit. He bowed politely to me and announced, *"Ich bin Prinz Albrecht von Bayern."*

To the horror of my family, I took this as an impossible joke, eyed him coldly, and answered, "Glad to meet you. Now may I introduce myself. I am the Queen of Sweden." And, as if that were not bad enough, I asked him to show his passport! The fact that we all sat talking around the empty table until two in the morning, and ended up with *"Auf Wiedersehen* in Salzburg!" is a tribute to the graciousness of His Royal Highness!

As we had found Germans in Buenos Aires, we found Austrians, Norwegians, Cubans and Egyptians in Venezuela. Aruba, Curaçao, and Bonaire speak a polyglot language called Papiamento, which confused us all hopelessly until we invented our own version, "Trappiamento." After that we managed nicely as far as Brazil, where Portuguese became a permanent mystery—to everyone but Father Wasner. Father "caught" Portuguese as others catch a cold or the measles. We had hardly put our feet on Brazilian soil when he seemed to talk the language fluently, though we had never heard a Portuguese word from him before. Johannes could not get used to it as he struggled along with Portuguese vowels. "Father goes up to a language, takes it by the halter, and pats its nose," he complained in his own pony slang, "then it nuzzles him."

Father's only comment to that was: "Well, I studied Latin for eight years, didn't I?"

In Trinidad we developed picturesque tropical diseases. Hester had an infected eye, and Lorli's leg suddenly swelled to the dimensions of elephantiasis. An Indian doctor who had studied in Vienna was found to treat the angry eye. He diagnosed Lorli's "piano leg" as an infection from poisonous coral she had stepped on at the Spanish Waters in Curaçao. "Well," said Lorli, eying her affliction, "at least this will make news for my next letter to Erika!"

But some of these "stings" were really, truly, sincerely *bites*, as we came to a closer personal knowledge of South American insect life: bugs, roaches, and giant mosquitoes making a noise like a siren. As for fleas—Lorli began to feel that single-handed she was keeping the species from extinction, while Agathe's face and arms looked like a relief map of southern Brazil. Only Johannes really thrived on it all, busily running a "catch-a-cockroach" contest against Father Wasner. The score in Rio was 15–13, with our dear priest-friend and conductor in the lead.

All these little irritations might years before have produced a real *Tropenkoller;* but we had never forgotten our Captain's lesson so we tried always to laugh over bites and stings, even when they could not be overlooked. Frequently one of us would find herself humming the Tyrolean *Echo Yodel* which, as an encore, always proved so successful on the stage. The words are definitely not polite (elegant version: "Be still, I shall leave when I am ready"; actual translation: "Shut your mouth, I go home when I want"), but they were wonderful for morale; and, as one after the other sang the little tune, we learned to pick it up all together and laugh our way through to the funny side of whatever was wrong.

Things went most really wrong in Curaçao on April nineteenth when Hester suddenly appeared, with round eyes and a serious face, to announce, "The Venezuelan Consulate is closed all day because of a national holiday." One great misery of the trip was that visas had to be obtained from one spot to another. We were to fly back the next morning to Caracas for our return engagement, and we needed a re-entry permit. Now the consulate was closed, to open only at nine the next morning—and our plane was leaving at eight. The situation was serious. Friends in Curaçao, the officials of K.L.M., the Austrian Consul, and the American Consul General all tried to intercede for us, but to no avail.

What were we to do? We wondered all through the concert that evening, and our greetings to backstage visitors must have been absent-minded. Suddenly, in the long line waiting, came a new face and a special introduction: "Mrs. Trapp, may I present the Consul from Venezuela?" . . . Every Trapp present froze into silence. In the surrounding quiet, the gentleman said, in Spanish, very much very quickly. Not a word about visas. He wanted autographs.

I tried a little joke: "We give autographs," I said, "you give visas." The Consul laughed merrily to show that he loved the joke—and shook his head.

Just then a formal invitation was handed to us for a party to be given immediately in our honor. "We will be pleased to accept," said Father Wasner, suddenly inspired, "if we may bring our friend, the Consul of Venezuela." I quickly got the point, took the Consul's "offered" arm, and let him "escort" me. For the rest of the evening we sat side by side, in the old Dutch mansion where the party was held, while the Consul spoke eloquently of music—Mozart's music, Beethoven's music, and his own music.

Whenever he paused, I said, "Visa."

Everyone present was most sympathetic. From time to time questioning eyes met mine, but always I had to shake my head, "Not yet." At midnight, after an emergency council of war with the family, Hester was dispatched to the hotel for our passports, while I made a public address to the Consul. Since midnight had officially ended the holiday, I told him, Hester would arrive shortly with the passports; and meanwhile we would sing for him—everything he wanted and everything we knew. Then, without giving him time for any comment at all, we began: first all the Spanish numbers we knew by heart; then Mozart's *Ave Verum* and *Ave Maria*; then the *Kyrie* from the *Missa Brevis*; then a gay round, *Freunde lasset uns beim Zechen*, then—then— At last there was Hester with the packet of green books.

By now the Consul had weakened just a little. "*Mañana a las siete*," he agreed. "Tomorrow at seven—and bring with you four additional photographs of each!" Then, smilingly, he bowed and withdrew. We looked at each other in fresh despair. It was almost too good to be true when our dear photographer-friend, Mr. Fischer, present at the party, saved the day by taking the pictures then and there. Leaving us to drink his health in Curaçao Triple Sec, he went home to develop and print them—and was back by 3:00 A.M., just in time for one last enthusiastic toast in his honor.

The plane was to leave at eight, and K.L.M. planes are famous for leaving on time. At a quarter to seven we were all outside the consulate. At a quarter past seven the doors were opened, and at seven-thirty the Consul arrived. Beaming, he carried—not our passports, but a sheet of music paper. Inspired by our singing, he told us, he had composed an entire *Ave Maria* after reaching home. In a minute we were deeply involved, with Father Wasner singing the *Ave Maria* at sight and the Consul happily beating time, while behind him the hands of a big clock swung slowly past seven-thirty. "I think we must leave," I said desperately; and, like one who is cruelly awakened from a beautiful dream, the Consul looked at the clock and sighed. A man was summoned. Seven-forty.

Suddenly, it was all accomplished, with passports stamped and goodbyes spoken. We were outside again, and Mr. Fischer was racing us to the airport. . . . Though all four of its motors were going, the plane was still on the ground. "*Vertragung* —delay," smiled the Dutch captain, then the door slammed behind us and the wheels taxied towards the runway. . . .

In Panama, after we had said goodbye to South America, the uncertainties of the world situation really caught up with us. As we landed at the airport, we were told that war had broken out in Korea and that American troops were already fighting. Now followed days of anxiety, while everyone around us talked gloomily of World War III. Werner was most worried about Erika's being in Austria, and Martina wondered whether Jean might want to return to Montreal. We knew that Rupert, as a doctor, could very possibly be drafted—and there we all were in Panama, still thousands of miles away from home.

The only memory I have of the Panama concert is that, during the last number before the intermission—it happened to be Johann Sebastian Bach's beautiful chorale, *Jesu Joy of Man's Desiring*—I saw Johannes stare fixedly at a given point on the stage. I followed his eyes. There, exactly above Father Wasner's head, was a huge scorpion at least five inches long, with its poisonous sting daintily and dangerously raised. . . .

The curtains had hardly closed when the evil-looking thing fell to the floor, and Johannes, armed with a handkerchief, pounced on his precious prey, and dashed off to preserve it in a handy bottle of cologne. The second half of the concert proceeded without incident, and for our first encore, we sang the *Echo Yodel*. Hedwig, our echo, disappeared into the wings, while I explained to the audience, as I always did, "I must apologize for the words to this song. They mean, 'I go home when I want.'"

"And," I thought firmly to myself, as Hedwig's first echo came back from the wings, "this time, *I want!*"

13

Saudade

After Panama, we flew to Mexico City, where we were invited by an old friend of ours, Sofía del Valle, to a Mexican dinner. We listened to her tell of the persecution of the Church in the 1930's, when she, with priests hidden in her house and Holy Mass being offered in her cellar, had been in constant danger of death. Sometimes the Blessed Sacrament had been entrusted to her care, and she had risked her life to bring it to condemned prisoners.

Then, as a fitting end to our stay and climax to our trip, we visited the pilgrimage shrine of Our Lady of Guadalupe and knelt in the big basilica before the image which the Madonna had miraculously impressed on the *tilma* of a poor Indian.

The last entry in my South American diary reads, without date: "Today we sing in Chihuahua and tomorrow in Monterrey. I am air-sick, sight-sick, homesick!"

At last came the home flight. Even the roar of the motors sounded different as our plane left the ground, and it was hard to believe that we had left the Southern Cross so far behind.

The most surprising thing of all was that the *mañana* tour had really worked out. We had given close to eighty concerts, most of them arranged on the spur of the moment, many of them unexpected return engagements at the request of the people. We finally understood why S. Quesada could not possibly have answered our anxious questions about "how many" concerts there would be, or in "which" countries we would sing . . . he really hadn't known. He was astonished and delighted at the outcome himself.

With any homeward trip can come the anxious question: "Have I been a good ambassador?"

Had we? I wondered. I thought back to a certain day in Caracas when Johannes had led Maria, Agathe, and myself to a small statue in an attractive little park. Curious, we went over to it and read: "Henry Clay, 1777–1852. Apostle for Fraternity among the Countries of America." Below, in smaller print, it said: "The United States of America gives this statue of its illustrious statesman, Senator and Secretary of State to the United States of Venezuela." Henry Clay, the Great Pacificator. Could we say as much—we, the Trapp Family, and the countless Americans we had met en route?

Certainly we had learned a great deal. When one has lived complacently in little Austria or little Vermont, a way of living can become *the* way of living, until one crosses a border. Traveling should be taken much more seriously as an instrument for world peace, I thought to myself in the plane. There is no better medicine for human cockiness and human pride. Traveling can teach humility—and without humility, national and individual, there can never be peace.

Of course, as far as our own trip was concerned, we had "heard" many things. Here and there reports would reach us that in such-and-such a town, after our concerts, the schools had begun to teach and sing old folk songs; or that such and such a bishop had spoken for an hour about the mission of music in the churches.

It is, nevertheless, a very sobering thing to be told that you have had an "influence"; and it brings straight home to your heart and conscience, as it did to me that day in the home-bound plane, the important question: "What kind of influence?" We felt a certain kinship with the great group of musicians who had appeared, and would appear, on the venerable stages of South America. We felt, too, that we were fulfilling a mission in traveling from place to place with our singing, but even if we had done something, we had not done enough. We had not even begun. One night after a successful concert, we had had to refuse eight requests for other engagements, just because of our own silly "surplus lack of time" (*Ueberfluss an Zeitmangel*), and I could not forget that choking-fig tree in the jungle outside Belém. That is why, for each one of us, the departure from South America was full of a very special and personal *saudade*. We could not wait to get home, but we could not bear to leave.

Our hearts were full as the sun set and darkness came down over our last glimpse of Mexico. I think I must have fallen asleep, because the slight shock when our wheels hit the runway came as a complete surprise.

Houston, Texas. Through my window I could see the airport attendants running forward with fuel and luggage trucks. Quickly we assembled our things and helped Johannes to organize. Then, as we stepped out of the plane, the whole sky seemed to be ablaze with rockets, rockets, and more rockets— a most wonderful display of fireworks. We had forgotten entirely—it was the Fourth of July!

We were Americans, and we were home.

14

Salzburg: 1950

We had less than a month at Cor Unum in that summer of 1950, as we were scheduled to sing in Austria at the Salzburg Festival on the eighth of August. The thought of returning "home" to the town we had so abruptly left as refugees held so many emotions for all of us that we put off thinking about it for as long as we could.

Besides, the dark clouds on the political horizon had not vanished. The war in Korea had not ended after two weeks, in spite of optimistic predictions. There were days during the month of July when it looked as though World War III might break out at any hour. Rupert, who knew about our plans for a European tour, left his busy doctor's office and came to Stowe, urging us to think it over carefully. Werner wondered anxiously whether he should cable Erika to return at once. I can still see us, the whole family, grouped around Father Wasner on the grass behind my little house at the camp. Father had read the newspapers carefully and followed the radio reports. He suggested that rather than make a hasty decision, we should wait a few more days. Finally we agreed; and when, after a few days, the crisis seemed to pass, we planned definitely to leave on the *Queen Mary*, August third.

As the date grew nearer, a growing excitement could be felt throughout the family. It was not the same kind, however, as we had experienced before setting out on the South American trip, when we were heading into the tropics for the first time. This visit would bring us again to Aigen-bei-Salzburg, our old home, after twelve years of absence and a most terrible war. How would we find it? Our thoughts and apprehensions and longings kept us preoccupied for the entire crossing. I can remember not one thing of that trip on the *Queen Mary* except that because of the Holy Year there were many American pilgrims on their way to Rome.

Our excitement deepened as the shoreline of Le Havre came in sight—and all but overwhelmed us when, finally, in Paris we took the night train for Salzburg. There were sleepless hours for more than one that night. The next morning we were in Switzerland. Then came the Austrian border.

Our return had been announced through radio and newspapers; and, at different stops of the Arlberg Express, beginning at Innsbruck, crowds were waiting on the platform to greet us. We had never seen these people before, but they knew of us through the Trapp Family Austrian Relief, since many of them had received medicines, food, coal, or clothing at the most critical time of their lives. Now they wanted to show their gratitude by cheering, as our train moved slowly into the station. We had had no idea of this and were deeply moved. As much as we could in the all-too-short minutes, we tried to tell them that we were only the instrument—that all those gifts had come from the generosity of the American people.

When the Express finally left Tyrol, and the mountains of Salzburg came in sight, the tension became almost unbearable. We knew every mile of that stretch—every peak, every village, every lone chapel and shrine. As we stood fearfully at the windows, some of us were praying, some were crying. Lorli and Maria held each other tight. Then we heard the long, familiar squeak of the brakes as the train took the wide curve at Gnigl—and there was Salzburg spread before our eyes, with the ancient Festung, its fortress, high upon a mountain, and the Salzach River, like a silver band, dividing the old town from the new. The train slowed down, slid into the station, and came to a halt. We had come home—to the land of Mozart and Schubert and *Stille Nacht*.

Outside, such a dense crowd pressed around the train that

I turned back from the window to say to Agathe behind me, "Look, there must be something going on today."

Hedwig said, "Mother, this is Festival time—don't you remember? There's something going on every day."

As we started to leave the train, a great cheer went up; and halfway down the steps, I said to Hester, "Someone important must be on this train—maybe Toscanini."

Then I heard Hester whisper softly in my ear, "I don't think those people are here to greet Toscanini—I think they are waiting for the Trapp Family."

It was true. As we stepped onto the platform we were suddenly and completely surrounded, greeted in the name of the city of Salzburg, and escorted to the main waiting room for the most touching welcome we had ever received in our lives. We met the new Archbishop, His Excellency, Dr. Andreas Rohracher; then the *Landeshauptmann* (Governor), the Mayor, and the children's orchestra from the Mozarteum. All rose from their seats as we were escorted in, and the children sang an Austrian song of welcome. There were representatives from the Austrian radio, speeches, and great bouquets of alpine flowers for each one of us; then the children played their instruments—and from the crowd pressing in around the station came again and again that rousing cheer.

At last we were led over to a waiting bus and—as the greatest surprise of all—driven past the hotels in town, past the town itself, across the bridge, and out to Aigen. There the bus slowed up at the gate of the Villa Trapp—now a seminary—drove over the familiar gravel of our own driveway, and stopped before the door we once had left. We had been invited, in the absence of the seminarians, away on vacation during the summer, to stay in our old home.

It was almost too much. Our hearts, after that unexpected welcome at the station, were full to bursting, and now this! All of a sudden we felt the heavy weight bear down on us— the weight of our special cross which was heavier today than it had been on any other day: that we returned without our Captain and father, who so long ago had led us on the flight into Egypt. Faith told us that he was closer to us now than he had been then, but—faith is a "dark light."

We were greeted at the doorstep by a most kind and friendly Father Rector, the Reverend Hermann Egger, who told us to make ourselves just as much at home as in the good old days, and gave us the key to the house, so that we might come and go as we pleased. Then he opened the door of the library, where tea was waiting—and there, looking down on us from the opposite wall, was a life-size picture of the Captain in Navy uniform. The first time I had seen him in uniform was at the altar on our wedding day, and after that he had always worn it for great family feasts. Once he had even mentioned casually that he would like to be buried in it. . . .

We had been told that many of our things had disappeared when our house was looted during the Nazi regime, and I had never thought to see that picture again. When I faced it now, eye-to-eye—the impact was so strong that all I could do was turn around and disappear in the general commotion. I ran upstairs to the chapel, where a flood of tears seemed to cleanse the soul, at least sufficiently to let it say again, together with Job, "Lord, Thou hast given him. Lord, Thou hast taken him. Lord, Thy name be praised."

Kneeling in the chapel, I prayed silently also for Father Wasner, who was bearing a similar cross. Relatives of his had come to the station to take him to his home, about two hours' ride from Salzburg. There he would go with his elderly mother to pray at the grave of his father, who had died during the war.

Though everyone was invited out by relatives and friends for this first evening in Salzburg, I remained at home, trying to put together the new and the old, the familiar and the unfamiliar. First I heard from Father Rector some details of the fate of the house since we had left it. Immediately after our departure in 1938, it had been confiscated by the Nazis and made into the headquarters of Heinrich Himmler. Father Rector showed me how the little private apartment Georg and I once shared had been modernized and turned into

Himmler's private quarters. He told me—what I already knew —that the chapel had been turned into a beer parlor with fitting murals painted on the walls. Three private telephone lines connected the house directly with Berlin, Berchtesgaden, and Vienna. I saw too where Himmler, in constant fear of being assassinated, had had a private, covered well dug for his own drinking-water. Our gracious park had been surrounded by a forbidding twelve-foot-high brick wall, and in the big meadows still stood several cabins that had been erected for Himmler's bodyguard.

Tears rolled down my cheeks as I realized that the whole last phase of that gruesome war had been conducted to a great extent from within the walls of this house—tears of horror at what had been done; tears of gratitude that we had been able to entrust our home forever to the missionaries of the Society of Precious Blood, the Order of our South American friend, Father Kraeutler. For all the crimes committed under its roof, today and every day Christ Himself is atoning on the altar.

For a long time I stood quite alone at the foot of the wide, curved oaken stairway, thinking back into the past. That space over by the door had once held thirty-two suitcases, lined up for the first concert tour—which, at that time, we thought would be the only one.

It was Lotte Lehmann who had really started everything. One summer day in 1936, Father Wasner had been teaching us some folk songs in the garden here at Aigen. Lotte Lehman, passing by outside, had overheard and had come in—to tell us that we had "gold" in our voices. She made us sing the next day in a contest in Salzburg. After that success, there came a brief radio appearance—to which Kurt von Schuschnigg, Chancellor of the Austrian Republic, happened to be listening. Because of him, we sang in Vienna, and because of Vienna, we made our "only" tour—departing with all our baggage through the very door that now stood half-open in front of me. . . .

Here, just by the window, on a certain memorable evening years before, Georg had waited for my return from a whirlwind visit to Reverend Mother Abbess at the Benedictine convent where I had once been a postulant. So often I had relived and retold the story. Now, suddenly, I seemed once again to be part of it. Out of the shadows, Georg's voice came back to my ears. . . .

"Well? Do you have an answer for me?" And there was my own voice, incredulous, wet with tears:

"They s-s-aid it would be right—that I should m-m-marry you!" There was the remembered sound of my own sudden weeping, and my head buried deep on his shoulder. . . .

There was I, some months before that, newly arrived as a governess, and standing at the foot of the stairs, while a family of motherless children came gravely down the stairs to meet me: Rupert, Werner, Agathe, Maria, Hedwig, Johanna, Martina. . . .

All over again, I heard the voice of the Bishop preparing me for marriage: "As second mother to these children, you will have all the burden and all the rights of the mother whom God has called. They are entrusted to you as if you had given birth to them, and you will have to answer before God's throne for every one."

Suddenly, into the midst of my memories, came the reality of Father Rector's voice calling from the library: "The family has come back, and we are all having a cup of tea together. Will you join us?" I had lived for an hour so intensely in the past that, when I entered the library, I instinctively looked for Georg's old, battered Austrian flag over the mantelpiece. We had all gathered below it on a fatal March night in the past, when, with tears in our eyes and voices, we had pledged that even if Austria could no longer live on the map, she would always live in our hearts. . . .

But the flag was gone, and there in the room was a giggling, chatting crowd—the Trapp Family, present, full of news of the past.

The days that followed were bitter-sweet. There were details to be planned and settled for the three concerts we were to give within the program of the Salzburg Festival: one *im grossen Mozarteumssaal;* the second on the big out-door stage in front of the Cathedral—a stage used up to that point only for performances of the mystery play *Everyman;* the third to be purely sacred music in the *Kollegien Kirche*—the University Church. Erika, in Salzburg since spring, had helped to make the preliminary arrangements.

A reception was given for us by His Excellency the Archbishop in the large aula of the University, with a moving address by the Archbishop himself. Then came a string quartet; a children's choir; and the *Platten-Lisei*—a well-known native poetess, reciting verses specially composed for that occasion. Afterwards we were presented with a bouquet of edelweiss as big as a small wagon-wheel. Carefully we treasured the precious, starlike little alpine flowers to take home to America, where they might be sent to at least a few of those who had so generously contributed to Austrian Relief.

As for Austrian Relief—at long last, we met up with our dear Father Nuwer, who so faithfully for the past years had distributed the bales and cartons we had been able to send. Father Saunders had already returned to the States and Cor Unum had known the joy of his presence. Father Nuwer was still in Salzburg with the American Occupation Forces in 1950 and invited us all to dinner at the Army Officers' Club—the eighteenth-century Schloss Klessheim outside Salzburg—where we ate American steak and American corn-on-the-cob in the golden splendor of a baroque ballroom. There were toasts and speeches, while Father thanked us and we tried to thank Father, who would take no credit at all. Instead, he introduced his right-hand man, a young sergeant, as having painstakingly shouldered all the work that went into the Austrian end of Trapp Family Austrian Relief.

"As fast as one bundle went out," said Father Nuwer, "three more would come in. Things got so that our man here practically had a nervous breakdown every time mail arrived from the Trapp Family!"

Back in Aigen, when word got round that the Austrian Relief had arrived in Salzburg, a small, constantly growing queue formed nearly every day outside the house. Nearly all were strangers. Some had come from a great distance; and each had his own story to tell, hoping we might be able to help. Even the most tragic situation can have its funny aspect. This was all too clear as, among the many cases of heartache and despair, there were also a few lorn maidens, young and not so young, who shyly but hopefully begged that we might find them a husband in America!

Meanwhile, though the truth did not came into focus until a few years later, Lorli had found a husband—American—in Salzburg. On a certain rainy day when all of us together made a pilgrimage up the steep hill outside the town to the shrine of Our Lady at Maria Plain, we were joined by an ex-Music-Camper, Hugh David Campbell. . . .

But that was part of the strangeness of everything. In our old home in Aigen, we were trying to put past and present together; and to make it harder, we were surrounded the whole time by friends from home in America. The Roger Putnams, our dear friends from Springfield, Massachusetts, were there; also three of our closest friends, seminarians from Washington, D. C.: Christopher Huntington, Paul Taggart, and Paul Fry—these last called Big Paul and Little Paul. Christopher and Big Paul had been good friends of the Captain.

Everyone was in Europe for the Holy Year, everyone had read *The Story of the Trapp Family Singers,* and everyone wanted to visit the Villa Trapp in Aigen. It seemed to us that little by little the entire traditional "first row" for the Chrismas concerts at Town Hall reassembled itself around us, and there were days when we literally did not know where we were.

We showed them Aigen, Salzburg, and Nonnberg, the Benedictine convent where I had been a postulant. We took a wonderful excursion, all of us together, for a festival week-end of music and folklore in Bergen-am-Chiemsee—where the music for Holy Mass, which Big Paul recorded on tape, was written to old peasant tunes with a zither accompaniment. There, too, we danced and sang our hearts out, even while an elderly Austrian gentleman, a distant relative of our family, stood disapprovingly some feet away and afterwards said to me coldly, "Why do you mix so with the common people?"

Then we discovered the Salzburger Heimatwerk, a co-operative store specializing in folk arts and crafts, and which had not existed before the war. We made friends with Tobi Reiser, the manager, and his musicians. Through them we found new treasures of folk art, folk music, folklore. One night the entire group came out to us at Aigen: Franzl, with his zither; Big Franz with the "Hackbrett"; others with harp, violins, and trumpets, till the walls resounded with beautiful music and Paul Taggart's tape recorder wound endlessly on and on into the night. . . .

Then there was the day of special homecoming—to Nonn-berg, the home of my heart, the Benedictine convent where I had once spent two happy years as an aspirant. Hearts opened wide together as we all met once again. Many pack-ages from the Austrian Relief had reached the Nonnberg, and I was asked to "say a few words," but I can only remember answering:

"Reverend Mother, all year long, everywhere, I make speeches and give little talks—but when a child comes home, there is no speech at all."

It was all so heart-rending and heart-warming that in the excitement we might well have forgotten to think seriously about the concerts—except that the very idea of them made us a little anxious. There were signs and rumors that the old feelings about our leaving Austria had not yet died out; that some people had heard and resented the fact that Rupert and Werner had fought in the American uniform.

On the day of the first concert in the Mozarteumssaal, Lorli woke up with a high fever; and Hedwig came down with an acute bronchitis. Both stayed in bed dosing themselves until the last minute. We were all nervous when finally we came on the stage.

As we sang our first number, the stage lights suddenly flickered and went out. It was a long time before an electrician could be found. Afterwards we learned that it was not by chance that the lights had flickered—even worse disturbances had been planned. We managed to complete the program; and at the end of the concert we sensed in the departing audience a spirit of peace and harmony.

The Domplatz concert in front of the Cathedral suffered from lack of publicity; but for the final "Hour of Sacred Music" the big Kollegien Kirche was filled to overflowing; and high up in the choir loft, we sang to thousands from the fulness of our hearts—with Mozart's *Ave Verum Corpus* the last number of all.

Afterwards, Tobi Reiser was waiting to invite us for another musical weekend—just what we needed. We met the "Riadinger Buab'm"—five young men whose singing brought tears to the eyes; and the "Fischenbachauer Dirndln," three girls who did just as well. We sang for them; they sang for us— while Big Paul recorded everything; Tobi played folk dances; and everyone joined in the dancing all afternoon, all evening, all the next day—until, late in the evening, we came back to the old house in Aigen.

There we discovered that Mr. Levitoff had arrived.

Mr. Levitoff was our manager for the European tour. The next day he made a formal call—erect, polite, with his walking-stick in his left hand—joining us for a cup of coffee as we finished our late lunch, to discuss the coming tour. Suddenly we realized that this really was a *concert tour*, and that the moment had come to leave Salzburg. Our three weeks were over, and no one knew where the time had gone.

After that everything went very fast. Erika's family urged her to join the trip and to let them keep Barbara until the end of the tour, so she hurriedly made preparations to come with us. Then came a last farewell to Nonnberg, and good-byes to His Excellency, the Archbishop—who, in that short time, had become a close, fatherly friend. One more cup of tea on the last evening with Father Rector, as our Captain in his Navy uniform watched us from the wall. One last glimpse, from the departing train, of the Festung and the ribbon of river dividing the city. Then we were on our way to Denmark.

Mr. Levitoff traveled with us; and as Salzburg disappeared in the distance, he drew out his bulging briefcase to speak of Scandinavia, France, and England.

15

Mr. Levitoff's Elephant

As the train rolled north across Germany, Mr. Levitoff took from his briefcase a small ivory elephant—a precious gift to him from Anna Pavlova, whose manager he had been for years. With a solemn face, he turned it around three times, explaining, "For good luck—each time we talk business." Then he began to outline the Scandinavian itinerary: "The first concert will be in Copenhagen . . . then ——, and after that —— Next, two concerts at ——" As Father Wasner leaned forward to concentrate on the details, I sank back into my corner. From a distance, I could hear Mr. Levitoff's voice saying: "Stockholm . . . correspondence with Mr. Börjegård . . ."

Once again I was overwhelmed by a rush of memories from the past. Mr. Eric Börjegård had been our manager and guardian angel during that anxious spring and summer of 1939, at a moment when we belonged neither to the old country nor to the new. Our first precious months in the United States had come to an end when our visitor's visas could not be renewed, so we had to go back to Europe to arrange a re-entry —strangers in our own land, refugees from Austria, feeling our way and praying that the way be shown. It was then that Mr. Börjegård arranged concerts for us in Copenhagen, Oslo, and Stockholm. I recalled, in 1950, the rising political tensions in July and August of 1939—how everyone talked about war and Father Wasner suddenly spoke Swedish.

Now, after all those years, we were heading once more towards Scandinavia, in a summer once again clouded with anxieties and talk of war. It seemed to me that we were again feeling our way from concert to concert and from country to country. The memory of Mr. Börjegård was very reassuring.

Little scraps and snatches of memories half-forgotten drifted through my head as the train rushed on: our brief visit at Falun with Selma Lagerlöf; Mother's Day in Assens, where Father Wasner had presented his choir with a beautiful new composition, *The Children's Blessing*—a song that has since found its way to many a mother's heart. We had sung it that day, all day long; and when evening came, Illi and Lorli both had the measles. . . . There was a concert at The Hague in a private home, and an "empty" concert in Olso, because the German Embassy, powerful in those days in the Scandinavian countries, had given out word that it was not "appropriate" to attend. . . .

By some hidden process of association, years dropped away in my mind, till Georg and I together were making that first memorable "tour" with our children way back in 1937. In London, we had had tea with Queen Mary, who discussed recorders with us in German, but obviously felt not the least bit attracted to what she called our "cunning little pipes." In Assisi, the holy village of Saint Francis, we had sung a volunteer concert for the poor, on a night so cold that we warmed our fingers over charcoal *scaldini* during the intermission. The whole thing turned into a musical fiesta, with the audience joining in every refrain; and, as our numb fingers played away on the recorders, out came a neat little cloud of vapor through the hole at the bottom of each. . . .

I could hear Georg's voice, on the farewell day of our stay in Rome, saying:

"I am very glad we took this trip."

Someone else had said that again years later, and in different surroundings. Was it I? Was it Father Wasner? . . . Across from me, as the train rattled over mild German countryside, Father Wasner sat reading his Breviary. Werner was at last finding time to give Erika the highlights of our South American adventures, and Mr. Levitoff had dropped off for a nap.

No, it was not Father Wasner, it was I myself—and suddenly my mind was back in Scandinavia in that dread September of 1939, with our passage to America still unsettled and a chilling announcement reaching everyone by radio, press, and phone: "Hitler has invaded Poland. There is war."

A cold fear had closed in then on all of us—for the fate of nations, for the fate of the world, and for ourselves. What if we might never return to America at all? All foreigners would soon be asked to leave Sweden, and we were refugees from Austria with almost no money. To make matters worse, Mr. Börjegård was obliged to tell us that of seventeen concerts lined up for us, all but six had been canceled.

We did the best we could. There was a church concert in Sigtuna, the old capital of Sweden—a concert in candle-light, while a lovely Madonna and a number of friendly saints smiled down at us from the carved medieval altarpiece—and, at the end of the concert, a most touching thing. The Lutheran pastor, who had been sitting in the first pew, came up the steps to the sanctuary, opened his arms wide, and embraced Father Wasner before his entire community. We could almost forget that a most terrible war had begun.

There was an hour of sacred music in the Cathedral at Upsala. Everyone was very moved, and the next morning came a most impressive visit to the Archbishop's house, where the Archbishop himself received us. We felt immediately drawn to this kindly, sympathetic, dedicated man, head of Sweden's twelve Lutheran bishops, who spoke to us of the "one Christian Church to which we all belonged" and of his hopes and prayers that all denominations might one day be united.

We sang for him then: a Bach chorale; the second *Agnus Dei* from the *Missa Brevis* by Palestrina; Mozart's *Ave Verum*; and a few Swedish numbers. Afterwards, the Archbishop referred to our mission and vocation—"which," he said, "is in your singing"; and at the end, he invited us to say "the prayer of Our Lord in the dear old language of the Church."

We all knelt, together with his wife, daughter, and household, as he began the Our Father in Latin. "*Adveniat regnum tuum*—Thy Kingdom come"—the words were very moving on that grave and anxious September morning; and a few days later, when news came that our American passage was finally arranged, there was only one thing to say. This time I myself was the one to say it:

"I am very glad that we could make this trip."

On September 26, 1939, we sang our last concert—in Karlstad—each one of us wondering, "Is it the last one forever? Will we ever come back?" And now . . .

There was a sudden hearty knock at the door of our train compartment; then the door slid open, and customs officials were upon us. We had reached the Danish border.

Late that evening, when the lights of Copenhagen finally came in sight, Mr. Levitoff stood up, politely trying not to disturb the knees of his fellow passengers. Solemnly he turned the little elephant three times around "for good luck." Then he restored it to a special section of his briefcase, next to a large picture of Anna Pavlova in a silver frame.

But something was definitely wrong. We reached Copenhagen to learn that Scandinavian managers did not think American standards could be applied to post-war Europe; that the prices asked were too high; and that several concert engagements had therefore already been canceled. Early the next morning, Mr. Levitoff knocked at Father Wasner's door to bring him some of the distressing correspondence—a great sheaf of letters, which Father, in his innocence, put down on the bed.

"Never do that!" exclaimed Mr. Levitoff, leaping to pick them up. "Never put business on a bed, or business will go to sleep!"

Father Wasner laughed, when he told us later of the little incident, but obviously, in our careless past, we had left too many letters lying on too many beds. Or else . . .

That European concert tour suffered really from two things: the time element and the lack of preparation. In 1950, too many big cities were still in ruins; too many bombed-out people were still without homes; and occupation armies were still everywhere. To make things worse—and here

was someone's error—advance publicity had tried to "sell" us
as "the greatest American box-office attraction of recent
years." This was, first of all, not true; and it meant that managers in the big cities rented the largest halls available, then
failed to fill them. How lovingly we thought back to the warm
spontaneity of South American methods, as day after day we
sang to "small but appreciative" audiences; because here in
Europe one bleak disappointment followed another while,
from one city to another, the little elephant tirelessly turned
and turned and turned. . . . Only in Wales, where we sang
to an audience of singers, did things really go well.

In Hamburg, the manager wanted jazz. In England, before
we had even half-completed our engagement, all further concerts were canceled. When another disaster occurred in Belgium, there was no longer enough money to pay us.

There was only one thing left to do, and from my very
modest little room in a small hotel in Paris, I did it. I placed
a person-to-person call to Freddy Schang in New York.

"Freddy," I said, across the thousands of miles, "could you
possibly, pul-leeze, cable us money for our passage home, as
an advance on our December concerts?"

Then my grateful ears heard Freddy's familiar, resounding
voice, bursting the transatlantic cable with a prompt and
heart-warming "Of course!"

16

Roma Aeterna

Rome was our consolation. We had already been there once, years before, on that famous "first tour." I remember that the monument to Victor Emmanuel—all white marble columns—had reminded me, at first sight, of a set of flashing false teeth. I remember that the Trapp Family Singers were allowed, in a large public audience, to sing Mozart's *Ave Verum Corpus* for a very frail and obviously dying Pius XI, who raised his arm in blessing with a gesture of tremendous physical effort. . . .

Things were different in 1950—in that holy, dedicated year when day after day hundreds of thousands of pilgrims crowded together into Saint Peter's, singing, "*Christus vincit, Christus regnat, Christus imperat.*" To Rome—to the Church of the Prince of Apostles, and to the living Vicar of Christ on earth—we took the disappointments, heartaches, and heartbreaks of our European tour.

Just before leaving home, we had heard much of the new excavations at Saint Peter's, revealing, we had been told, the exact spot where the Saint lay buried. Would we—would we be able to visit the excavations? As Victor Emmanuel's gleaming dentures shot once again past our plunging taxi, I prayed with all my heart. . . .

Our first visit was to elderly Archbishop Birretti, a canon of Saint Peter's Basilica, whom we had met a few weeks before in Salzburg.

"Welcome, welcome!" The Archbishop seemed filled with genuine pleasure at seeing us. "What can I do for you?"

Casually but confidently, I took the plunge. "Your Excellency, we would like very much to see the new excavations —especially Saint Peter's tomb."

The kindly face before us became almost helpless, and the Archbishop threw up his hands in a gesture of despair and anguish. "No, no!" he said hastily. "*Impossible—impossible!*"

And why?

Still agitated, he explained. Even he, Archbishop Birretti, had not yet been permitted to view the excavations. Monsignor Ludwig Kaas, the German-born Administrator of Saint Peter's, had absolute charge of the proceedings, and he was *un huomo molto difficile.*

"*Numquam ridet,*" added Archbishop Birretti, as if Latin might be more emphatic. "He never laughs."

I tried again: "Your Excellency, perhaps you would telephone to him and ask permission for us." The Archbishop merely gave me a long, pitying look. Silence.

"Then we will go in person," I said, "if Your Excellency will kindly make the appointment." At least Monsignor Kaas could do no more than say no.

His Excellency considered me with a mixture of admiration and deep prophetic gloom. "*Aspetti un momento,*" he said, and reached for the phone.

Very soon a youngish-looking priest entered the room. "Please," said the Archbishop, and his voice was eloquent, "accompany the Signora Trapp to the Palazzo San Carlo and introduce her to Monsignor Kaas."

Was it only my imagination, or did the friendly, smiling countenance of the young priest really fall when he heard his assignment? By now, I was getting curious. I took leave of His Excellency and the family, promising to be back soon.

My young guide, Monsignor Toth, was quite talkative as he led me out of the Palazzo Santa Marta, where Archbishop Birretti lived. When we neared the Palazzo San Carlo, deeper within the Vatican Gardens, however, he became more and more silent. At last we knocked on the door of a beautiful Renaissance building—and waited. Monsignor Kaas was not at home.

"Let's go—he is not here," said my escort, whirling on his heels with tremendous relief in his voice.

"But perhaps he will be here soon," I protested. "We have come all this way. What a shame to miss him by a few minutes!" I began to talk rapidly about America and our life as concert singers, while poor Monsignor Toth looked right and left with unquiet eyes, obviously hoping that I might soon give up the whole idea.

Suddenly, with no warning, *he* was bearing down on us —a tall figure in cassock and wide-brimmed Roman sacerdotal hat. Monsignor had just time to whisper, "Address him as 'Your Excellency'!"—when six feet of darkness stood towering over me.

"What do you want?" said His Excellency sharply in German.

My guide stammered a few introductory words—then once again I plunged. In a few rapid sentences I managed to explain who we were, how we had reached America, and why we were now in Rome. I finally landed at the whole question of the new discoveries at Saint Peter's and ended up with ". . . and so here I am to ask Your Excellency's permission: please, may we visit the excavations?"

There was an ominous, empty silence. Then His Excellency said in a glacial voice, "*What* excavations?"

If Monsignor Toth had suddenly started to sing *Old Black Joe* or the whole Palazzo San Carlo had begun to walk away, I couldn't have been more astonished. The answer sounded so much like a joke to me that I decided to join in the joking. "Oh, hasn't Your Excellency heard?" I laughed. "There are some new excavations at Saint Peter's that are now attracting world-wide attention. We are hoping to visit them tomorrow—tomorrow morning. We are going to have Mass in the crypt of Saint Peter's, and we thought that afterwards would be a splendid time to visit the excavations. . . . We shall sing during the Mass—Palestrina, Lasso, and Vittoria.

Does Your Excellency like sixteenth-century music? Your Excellency is most heartily invited. . . ."

Then I held my breath. Storm clouds—with thunder, lightning, and gunfire—seemed to rise and swirl and sink and settle over the palazzo. When "it" was over and the smoke had cleared, the three of us were still standing—and, of all things, Monsignor Kaas was saying that he "might be there." But he made no promises.

The next morning Archbishop Birretti, in surplice and purple cassock, met us at the entrance to the crypt and guided us downstairs to an altar, looking more than doubtful as we told him of the invitation I had issued. There was no one in sight.

The crypt of Saint Peter's—also a burial place for some of the popes—is low-vaulted. As we started the *Kyrie* from Palestrina's *Missa Brevis*, it sounded powerful and indescribably beautiful. After Holy Mass had ended and all of us had made our thanksgiving, we were so taken by the gloriousness of sound in this vaulted subterranean room that we continued to sing. Then—slowly, from behind a pillar, emerged a tall figure in a black cassock. It was Monsignor Kaas. He strode over to Father Wasner and pronounced one single word: "Excellent!"

Behind me, Archbishop Birretti suddenly whispered audibly and excitedly, "*Ridet—ridet!*—He smiles—he smiles!"

It was true. The awesome Administrator of Saint Peter's was smiling all over his face. And then—the incredible happened. Monsignor Kaas, still smiling, produced his keys and beckoned us to follow—down, down, into the mysterious grottoes below the crypt. The dim light revealed richly colored stucco work, funeral niches, coffins, an alabaster urn. Our guide led us through a long passageway, explaining as he went the significance of stones or murals or ancient columns. As his keys opened one door after another, we went from treasure to treasure of the pagan and early Christian world.

At one point Father Wasner stopped to read aloud a finely carved inscription on a stone in the floor: *Dormit in Pace—* Sleep in Peace.

Behind me I heard Hedwig asking, "Where is Saint Peter?" According to Christian tradition, Saint Peter is buried at a spot somewhere below the main altar of the great basilica. Had the excavations really proved this to be so? Eagerly we waited to hear.

But Monsignor Kaas, for reasons of his own, did not answer the question directly. Instead, he suddenly opened a massive bronze gate and motioned us all to step through. All at once we found ourselves in the *Confessio*—in the holy spot to which the Pope and his cardinals come once a year, on the Feast of Saints Peter and Paul, for silent prayer. We knew that we were directly under the main altar of the church. As Monsignor Kaas followed us in, he made a solemn, meaningful pronouncement:

"Here you are standing at the tomb of Saint Peter—and now, *sing*."

There was a breathless moment of silence, then a quick consultation. We chose King John of Portugal's *Crux Fidelis*, and we *sang*—in honor of the death by crucifixion that Saint Peter had shared with his beloved Master. . . .

Then, from the tomb of Christ's first Vicar, we came into the presence of Pius XII, His Vicar on earth. There was to be a public audience in the great church above our heads, and the Archbishop had arranged for tickets. From our high seats we could look down the full length of the nave as the pilgrims entered—hundreds of thousands of pilgrims from all over the globe, entering in procession and singing in their native tongues. For a long period of waiting we listened to one national song after another—then, suddenly, an inexplicable electric current of feeling went through the entire multitude. Someone intoned *"Credo in Unum Deum"*—the third Credo in Gregorian chant. Like thunder it rose, taken up throughout the entire church in one great unity of voice and spirit.

Even before the last "Amen" came the first distant shouts of *"Eviva il Papa! Eviva il Papa!"*—and we knew that the Holy Father was on his way. Far down the nave we could see

him coming—his chair, the *sedia gestatoria,* borne above the
heads of the multitude. Then the Holy Father was standing
—a tall, white, almost transparent-looking figure—standing
with arms outstretched as though he would draw us all to his
heart. From the throne he addressed all his children, warmly
and paternally, in Italian, French, English, Spanish, and German. Then came the solemn moment. Pius XII rose to his
feet, and a deep vibrant silence settled over the multitude.
Slowly the Holy Father raised his eyes to Heaven and pronounced the words of the Apostolic Blessing, making the sign
of the Cross in all four directions. There were tears on many
faces, but no sound—no words. There were no words to say.

We were silent for long afterwards, even when the great
basilica was empty and the vast piazza outside streaming
with the thousands who would now go their separate ways.
We did not even speak as we passed the great obelisk that
marks the spot of Saint Peter's crucifixion and saw, cut firmly
into the enduring stone, the six triumphant words, "*Christus
vincit, Christus regnat, Christus imperat.*"

It was some time later, and our feet had nearly taken us
home across the Tiber, when Martina finally broke the silence. "I don't think I'll miss Austria when we leave Europe,"
she said, "but I'm homesick for Rome already."

So at last we sailed for home, grateful with all our hearts
to Freddy Schang, who had sent us the return passage. The
trip had been a real pilgrimage, a journey of faith through
joy and heartache. In our own city, we had found sadness
and gladness. In the cities of others, we had been turned
away. In the Eternal City, we had sung for Saint Peter and
received the blessing of Pius XII. Now we were going home.

Standing at the rail in the cold November twilight, I
watched the *Liberté*'s bow cutting into the open sea. For a
moment my thoughts went back to Salzburg—to Father Rector's library and the life-size portrait; then mind and heart
took fresh direction. "I wonder," I thought, "if the ship's lantern in the cemetery at Cor Unum has been kept trimmed
and filled?"

As if to answer my question, the *Liberté*'s starboard light suddenly flashed on and burned unwinkingly through the dusk—a small happening, but for me it was more than reassuring. "Just the same, Georg," I said firmly into the ocean darkness, "I'm very glad we took this trip."

17

Brother Dutton and Bishop Lane

When Georg and I were first married, we spent many an evening at home in Austria talking about the future of the children. In those days, between World War I and World War II, my husband did not at all like the political look of things and seemed to have a sixth sense of what the future might bring.

"Terrible things are coming," he kept saying. "We should try to get out while we still can."

One day he made a surprising suggestion: "Let's sell everything here. Let's buy a yacht and go to the South Seas."

"For how long?" I asked, more than astonished.

"What do you mean, 'for how long?' For good, of course."

Still I did not take him seriously. "But, Georg," I protested, "what about school for the children? Are we to take teachers along?"

"Certainly not. Schools waste too much time anyway. You and I can teach them everything they need."

"All right, Georg." Pause. "But what about when they grow up and want to get married?"

"Well, what about it? With those beautiful islanders, they couldn't do better!"

With this my husband touched the very limits of my ability to understand. Could he really think that his daughters and sons might marry those . . . those . . . "But, Georg—" I said. Then words failed me, and I simply walked out of the room.

The discussion ended, but not for long. Patiently, time

and again, Georg kept returning to his favorite idea; and, inch
by inch, I felt myself weakening. All right, we *would* buy a
yacht; all right, we *would* make a trip around the world; but
—and here I held firm—we would *not* burn every last bridge
to the mainland. So finally there came a compromise: I agreed
that we should all set sail together into the South Pacific;
and Georg agreed that perhaps we should not sell the house
until we saw how well we liked it there.

The next thing was to find a boat. For days we inspected
yachts, yawls, schooners—even a beautiful four-master. Georg
was in his element, looking at all of them with the eyes of a
professional seaman. At the end of two weeks he announced
what was wrong with each boat, and decided that our
schooner must be built to order. That was in March, 1935. In
June a shipbuilder came to Salzburg with blueprints, while
everyone in the family caught "South Sea fever" and began to
read and talk Polynesia. On Pentecost Monday, Georg gave
final orders to proceed with the construction. I had never before seen him so happy.

Then suddenly it happened—we had no money. I have already told about that in *The Story of the Trapp Family
Singers*. All building was interrupted. "Postponed," said
Georg hopefully. When Austria was invaded, there was still
no boat, so the plan of many years had finally to be canceled.

"We were too late," said Georg sadly, and I felt guilty.
Without my opposition we might all have been safe on some
little green island where, as my Captain used to say in those
pre-war days, "no war would ever reach."

Years later, his dream for us came true.

During the second war, one of our concert tours took us
to Beloit, Wisconsin. After a tiring overnight train trip, we
learned at the hotel desk that the rooms we had reserved
were still occupied, so there was nothing to do at that early
morning hour but establish ourselves in the lobby for a long
wait. Just as we were settling down, however, the hotel door
swung suddenly open and a priest entered, hurrying towards
us with outstretched arms.

"Welcome!" he beamed. "Welcome to Beloit! We have all looked forward so impatiently to meeting the family from Brother Dutton's town!"

"From whose town?" We looked so completely blank that it was the priest's turn to be puzzled.

"But if you are the Trapp Family, you come from Stowe, Vermont, don't you?"

Yes, we did.

"Well, then, you must know much more about Brother Joseph Dutton than we do here."

We had to admit that we had never heard the name.

Our new friend shook his head slowly. "Well, well, well!" he marveled. "To think that here in Beloit we have a Brother Dutton Memorial School! To think that, for that school, I made a trip across the country to Stowe, Vermont. I even brought back a piece of wood from the old beams of the little red farmhouse where Brother Dutton was born—but the Trapp Family Singers of Stowe, Vermont, have never heard the name!"

Obviously, it was high time for the situation to be straightened out; and a few minutes later we were all gathered around a table in a nearby coffee shop as the priest began our education.

"Let me begin at the beginning," he said. "You must have heard of Father Damien, the priest of the lepers of Molokai."

Thank God—yes—we knew of him.

"Then perhaps you know that in 1886, two years before Father Damien himself caught the dread disease, a tall and handsome man appeared at Molokai, announcing that he had come to help at the leper colony. This man was Brother Joseph Dutton— Are you sure that nobody has told you of him?"

Silence. We had to conclude that people back in Stowe didn't know too much about Brother Joseph. "Did he live in Stowe all his life?" asked Agathe. "I mean, until he went to Molokai?"

No, Father explained, Brother Joseph had been born in Stowe but brought up in Wisconsin. During, and after, his few married years he had led a merry, wild life; then, on his

fortieth birthday, he had been received into the Catholic
Church. At that time he changed his earlier name of Ira for
a new one, "Joseph—because," as he says himself, "of Saint
Joseph, who led me straight into the arms of the historic
Church to enjoy its great penitential system."

For some time the new Joseph searched for the form his
penance would take. At first, he thought his place might be
with the Trappists in Kentucky; but finally, still looking for
his true vocation, he came across an article on Father Damien
and the lepers of Molokai. Suddenly, Brother Joseph knew
where God wanted him. He purchased a one-way ticket to
Honolulu and obtained permission to enter the leper colony
as a helper to Father Damien.

"Forty-five years later," said our narrator, "he was buried
there."

It was a touching story—that account of the leper colony
with its priest-father, a leper himself, supported and sus-
tained by a determined New Englander from our own state.
At the concert that evening, we were proud and pleased to
be introduced—not as the Trapp Family Singers, but as the
"people from Stowe, Vermont, where our Brother Dutton
was born." "Our Brother Dutton"—these Wisconsin people
spoke as though he really belonged to them more than to
Stowe; and I remember that I felt a little jealous, although
only a few hours before I had not even known the name.

"We have a good friend in Stowe who knows everything,"
I told our priest friend as we said goodbye. "Perhaps he can
tell us more about Brother Joseph."

So it happened that, not too long afterwards, back in
Stowe, we went to call on Uncle Craig Burt.

"What do you know," we asked, "about someone named
Joseph Dutton?"

Uncle Craig looked thoughtfully at the ceiling. "I used
to write to him," he said—and a few minutes later we were
looking at the faded souvenirs of a past correspondence. There
was a colored post card of the leper settlement: a church,
a row of cabins, some trees and shrubs, a forbidding wall of
rocks. There was an enlarged snapshot with an inscription:
"Joseph Dutton to Vermont friends." There was a letter:

"Dear Mr. Burt . . ." and, most impressive of all, a dim photograph of Brother Joseph Dutton at the age of eighty-seven. We looked into the face of an old man—a wonderfully alive face framed in bushy white hair and a long beard. Most remarkable, however, were the deep-set eyes under the prominent forehead—smiling, kindly eyes, but eyes which somehow gave the impression of having more than once thrown a glance into hell itself. . . .

It may not have been pure coincidence that our pastor in Stowe, Father McDonough, had also stumbled over Brother Dutton's name and become interested. "It's a shame he is so little known," Father said to us one day. "One should do something about it."

Little by little, through the slow passage of time, Father began to do something about it. First, land was purchased —near the site of his birth—from Joseph Dutton's relatives. Next, white pine, Vermont marble, and beveled glass were brought together for the construction of the Brother Dutton Memorial Chapel just outside Stowe Village. The celebrated painter, André Girard, decorated it outside and in. At last it was finished. When the time came for the dedication of the altar, our Captain had left us. The rest of us, however, will always feel close to this "skiers' chapel," where we so often have sung the High Mass for Christmas and Easter. Now and then Rosmarie has taken her paint brush to repair a weathered fragment. Martina was married there in 1949; and it was from Brother Joseph's chapel that we carried her, on a cold February day in 1951, to sleep beside her father in the freshly broken earth at Cor Unum.

During the summer of 1951, the Trapp Family Music Camp was honored by a visit from Bishop Lane of the Maryknoll Fathers. It was the fifteenth of August, the Feast of the Assumption—with over one hundred and fifty people present for the Liturgical Sing Week.

After lunch, the Bishop was led to speak of his experiences in Communist concentration camps in China; and, as we begged him to continue, he went on to give a most interesting and inspiring description of missionary activities throughout the world. Hours went by as minutes, while we alternately laughed and cried.

"Bishop Lane," some one of us said, "couldn't we go to the missions, too? Couldn't we do something for them? Couldn't we sing for them?"

I can still see how Bishop Lane whirled round in his chair. "Would you really want to do that?"

The whole beautiful day seemed to focus and hang suspended on his question.

"It could be arranged," he added quickly. "Where would you like to go? Japan? The Philippines? Hawaii?"

We thought of Brother Dutton. In the few seconds that followed, there was no time to say yes or no. There was only time to chorus, "Hawaii!"

So Hawaii it was. In no time the Bishop had got in touch with his own missioners, and they had approached Mr. and Mrs. George Oakley, the best-known concert managers in Honolulu. The Oakleys then approached Freddy Schang—and, suddenly, it was all arranged. We were told that we were to be in the Islands for three weeks in March, 1952.

Father McDonough suggested that he come with us for the trip—and come he really did, flying out to join us in Los Angeles when the time came.

Together we boarded the *Lurline* for our sea voyage: Monsignor Wasner, Father McDonough, and the rest of the "people from Stowe"—Agathe, Maria, Hedwig, Lorli, Werner, Johannes and myself. Our destination was at long last to be that northernmost group of islands in the South Seas which Georg had referred to as the Sandwich Islands. I remembered his voice, in the remote time of our past planning, saying, "For good, of course."

But it was not to be for good. We would return—to Georg, our Captain; and to Martina; to Rosmarie and Erika and Barbara and baby Martin, who waited for us at Cor Unum. Meanwhile, we carried with us a great wreath of fir and balsam as a present from Stowe, Vermont, for Brother Joseph Dutton.

He had long since become a very good friend.

18

Aloha

Weeks were to pass, however, before we could set foot on Molokai. As the *Lurline* carried us peacefully over the water, we learned three things: (1) *aloha*; (2) how to eat the pasty Hawaiian dish of poi; (3) how to refuse, firmly, ever to eat poi again.

Then, on a radiantly sunny morning, we came into Honolulu. An hour before docking, the *Lurline* was met by a boat bringing port authorities, immigration officers, doctors—and visitors; with the result that, as we stood by the rail watching Diamond Head, we were suddenly surrounded, hung with garland after garland of fragrant blossoms, and —it seemed to me—kissed from all directions at once. Mr. Oakley had brought a whole armful of leis. A lady from the Women's Club carried another, sent by the Maryknoll Sisters. Each greeting brought an aloha and a kiss, which Father McDonough gallantly braved, while Johannes turned and fled. As for Monsignor Wasner: "Maybelle!" we heard him cry to someone who had just adorned him with a beautiful carnation lei, and whom he quickly introduced as "my first English teacher!" Maybelle, it seems, had been a young American tourist during Father Wasner's first summer as an ordained priest on a Tyrolean mountain lake, and they had exchanged language lessons. Now, here she was.

"Teaching Spanish at the University of Hawaii," explained Maybelle.

Just then the *Lurline* neared the Aloha Tower and a band

ashore began playing *"Aloha Oe."* "Aloha" was really the
word. Everyone on board ship to whom we said goodbye answered with "Aloha," and everyone who wanted to bid us welcome to the islands said, "Aloha." We quickly acquired the
habit, too.

That one first night in Honolulu seemed like a dream, all
set to the music of unfamiliar words like "Waikiki" and
"papaya" and *"mahimahi."* We learned that "ti-leaves" do not
make a beverage, and how to say Queen Liliuokalani. I remember that, after supper, Maybelle had us all driven by car
up the Tantalus, a peak in the mountain chain behind Honolulu, so that we could look down on the whole city stretched
out through the night in a wide semi-circle of sparkling lights.

Next, we were all back in Maybelle's apartment, being
shown some glorious colored slides. "Every island has its
own official flower," she explained, as we watched "yellow
shower trees," "pink shower trees," "silver swords," and feath-
ery blossoms in deep red.

"What," Father McDonough asked, "is the official flower
for Molokai?"

"The kukui blossom"—and a creamy white flower, strong
and fragile at the same time, appeared suddenly on the
screen.

Once again Father McDonough's wistful voice came out
of the dark. "Do you have a picture of the leper settlement
on Molokai?"

"No, not of the settlement itself. No one is allowed to go
there without a special permit from the health authorities,
and they are not easy to obtain."

This was news. There was a short silence during which
we all faced possible disappointment. I thought, too, of our
wreath of Vermont balsam twigs, and I could feel Hedwig
fervently hoping that we might not have to carry it home
again.

"But," said Maybelle, "I can show you a picture I once took
from the air as we circled over Molokai."

And again we found ourselves looking at that steep, gloomy

mountain that Uncle Craig had shown us on a post card from
Brother Dutton.

"This is the pali of Molokai," Maybelle explained. "The
tall rock grows straight out of the ocean, and that little three-
cornered white speck at its foot is Kalaupapa, the peninsula
with the leper settlement."

As we looked, fascinated, she began to pack up the slides
and close the box. "*Pau*—that's enough," she said firmly. "You
have had a long day."

So we all separated for the night. Mr. Oakley had arranged
for us to stay in private homes because of a hotel strike at
the time. Gratefully, we retired. I remember how Johannes
made sure the wreath was safe in a box under his bed; and
how, late as it was, I wrote two letters with the same request:
one to the Bishop and one to the health authorities.

KAUAI

Mr. Oakley had told us that we would tour the Islands before returning for our big concert in Honolulu; so the next
morning we left by plane for Kauai, with leis around our
necks and leis dripping from our arms. The delicately scented
flowers made a festivity out of things one might otherwise
simply have "done"; and, as we rose high in the air above our
diamond-necklace city, we realized for the first time that
"aloha" can mean not only "farewell," but also "till we meet
again."

Our only companion on the plane was a native Hawaiian
lady—three hundred pounds of round darkness—whose name
was not, as I had been led to expect it might be, "Girl-who-
came-when-the-full-moon-was-rising-behind-the-mountain," or
"She-whose-beauty-is-bright-as-the-sea." This lady's name was
simply Mrs. Stewart. She had married an Englishman. She
told us, too, that she had once danced at the court of Queen
Liliuokalani. . . .

Then in no time wheels came down to meet the runway,
and we were in Kauai, being met by Father Remy and Mrs.
Ching. We were all promptly buried once again in leis and
kisses. Johannes' snub nose disappeared in fragrant blossoms;

and only his blue eyes could be seen, looking straight ahead, as he tried bravely to maintain his original premise that this was all "girls' stuff."

Next we were whisked up a winding mountain road towards the Kalalau lookout into the Waimea Canyon, for a picnic lunch of rice and poi and chicken served up in coconut shells by Mrs. Ching and her helpers, with a ti-leaf tablecloth and dark red *lilikoi* juice from the fruit of the passion flower. On the way down we stopped beside the gleaming white sand of Poipu beach, while Father Remy hailed a tall, bronze-skinned Hawaiian who had just shouldered his surf-board. He was introduced, though not as "Watchful-one-who-rides-like-a-swan-on-the-crest-of-the-wave."

"Mr. Schimmelpfennig, this is the Trapp Family," said Father Remy. Mr. Schimmelpfennig's mother had married a German.

Mr. Schimmelpfennig was only too glad to let us use his surf-board, and each one of us in turn tried to come in on the breakers.

Then, much too soon, sounded Father Wasner's warning voice: "Don't forget, we have a concert tonight!"

And what a concert it turned out to be. Father Remy had said there would be no *haoles*—members of the white race—present. Mrs. Ching had painted the backdrop with her art pupils from the local high school. We were a little uncertain before this, our first concert in the Islands, as to whether the Polynesians would like Palestrina, Mozart, and the mountain calls of Austria.

We need not have worried. After the first group, all our fears disappeared. Enthusiasm in the audience rose through the selections of Gregorian chant and the *Missa Brevis* of Palestrina; and, when we ended with Father Wasner's new arrangement of *Aloha Oe*, everyone rose as for a national anthem. Father Remy was very happy, and we felt solemn and elated.

The next day there was a concert for school children, little ones—Japanese, Chinese, and Filipinos—each trotting out with a rolled-up mat under his arm, then squatting on it in grave earnestness to listen to the singing. They looked like lovely little dolls, with round hair-cuts and eyes like big black Bing cherries. The evening concert was for high school children; and we were touched by their earnest attention, genuine enthusiasm, courtesy, and real discipline, such as we had hardly ever met in any high school on the mainland.

When the last suitcase of concert equipment had been packed, the last autograph given, and the last glowing eyes had disappeared, Father Remy said, "Now we go to the Kauai Inn. I have a surprise for you."

He had already told us much of the Polynesians and the ancient "chanters" whose singing preserved from generation to generation the history and genealogy of the people. What was coming?

To our amazement, the surprise was none other than our friend, Mrs. Stewart—Mrs. Stewart who had danced at the court of Queen Liliuokalani. With her daughter and granddaughter, she sang several of the quaint old chants, accompanied from time to time by beating on gourds. Then on a torch-lit stage under an old banyan tree the three started to dance—the sacred hula. Suddenly, magically, our friend's three hundred pounds turned into pure grace and fluid motion, with hands and fingers telling eloquently of rain, fear, longing—the whole story of a human heart. We did not need to understand the words of the chant: we were living in a fairy-tale. . . .

The next morning half of our audience was at the airport. "I'm sorry I don't have the neck of a giraffe," mumbled Johannes over a thick layer of carnation leis. His distaste seemed to have vanished. When the time came to board the plane, we sang *Aloha Oe*, while everyone listened with quiet intentness, and tears on many faces, our own included.

Johannes was the last one to enter the plane; and, before ducking through the low door, he stopped to call back in a ringing voice, *"Mahalo nui loa!"*

"That means, 'Thank you very much,' Mrs. Stewart's granddaughter told me," he explained to Lorli, as the plane took off. "Say, she has a Hawaiian name, Kaililauokekoea. It means: 'The-beautiful-one-with-skin-as-soft-as-the-koa-leaf.'" In the same breath, he added, "I have twenty-eight. How about you?"

He meant leis.

Lorli had thirty.

MAUI

The next stop was the island of Maui, and on the way we flew over Molokai. With our own eyes we saw the steep, rocky cliffs, and almost—almost—we could make out the clustered buildings of the leper settlement. As we looked down in silence, I saw Father McDonough solemnly make the sign of the Cross, as a blessing on the spot.

"Brother Dutton," I heard Hedwig call, "we are coming with a surprise for you." Or so we hoped.

At the Maui airport we were met by the Maryknoll Sisters, some of their school children and members of the local concert committee. Alohas—kisses, leis—while plans were quickly completed for our visit to the missions the next day and for a concert to be given that night. Then, suddenly, we were all being whisked off in various cars to watch a sunset from the top of the Haleakala, the largest dormant volcano in the world. Johannes, Lorli, Maria and I found ourselves in a convertible driven by a young woman who introduced herself as Mrs. Rocket, urged us to call her Natalie, and hoped we wouldn't mind if we stopped by for a moment at her house so she could give a quick supper to her little boys.

Then came the scene-of-the-month. As the convertible drew up in front of a beautiful modern home, two little boys, aged perhaps six and four, came shooting out of the house with cries of "Mommy! Mommy!" Big tears rolled down the cheeks of the smaller one.

As Natalie dropped everything to take him in her arms, we heard her say, "What's the *pilikia*, Johnny? Does your *opu* hurt?"

Johnny shook his head, sobbing bitterly. Finally he got out, "Danny says I'm *lolo!*"

The young mother seemed relieved. "Oh, come, this is only a *pilikia lii lii*, not a *pilikia nui*," she said soothingly. "Remember, you are Mama's *keiki kane*, and Danny is *lolo* himself. Danny—" and she coralled the older one with a firm hand —"you make me *huhu*. What will the ladies think? I'm *hila hila!*"

Danny looked contrite.

"Have you done your homework?" his mother continued. "No? Now, Danny, *wikiwiki hana pau*, before you can take your bicycle. Understand?"

Danny apparently understood. We did not.

Meanwhile, as she dealt out these admonitions, Natalie had produced supper for the two little boys. With a final, "Come. *Hele mai ai!*" she helped little Danny into his chair, murmured reassuringly, "*Pilikia pau*—now, boys, Daddy will be home any minute," and was back in the car. Two small faces smiled through drying tears, four little hands waved from the verandah—and we were off.

Promptly we flooded Natalie with questions: "What is *huhu?*" "What is *opu?*"—till Natalie laughed so that she could hardly drive, and called us "real *malihinis.*"

"Real *what?*" we chorused.

"Real new-comers to the island."

"And what does that make you, Mrs. Rocket?"

"I am a *kamaaina*—I live here," she announced proudly.

"Are you still *huhu?*" asked Johannes from the rear.

"No." Natalie laughed. "*Huhu* is 'angry,' but I should be *hila hila*—'ashamed,' because I shouldn't have teased you for not understanding the funny mixed-pickles we talk here."

"What does *pilikia pau* mean?" Lorli asked. "You said it several times."

"*Pilikia* means 'trouble,' and *pilikia pau* is 'now the trouble is over.' You might just as well get used to some of these words. You will be hearing them all the time you are in the islands. An *opu* is a 'stomach,' and *wikiwiki hana pau* means 'quick, finish your work.'" Natalie laughed again. "When I went home last Christmas with the children to visit my parents in Oklahoma, I complained to my mother that it was very hard to teach the children good English, because they learned such a mixture from other children. My mother answered, 'It wouldn't be so hard, if you would speak English yourself!'" . . .

And then, starting at sea level, we were on our way up the Haleakala. The road climbed steadily through the bluish greens and the reds of the pineapple fields, then reached a stretch of crippled-looking pines with gnarled branches that reminded us of Austrian *Latschen,* or the mugo pines in our own garden in Vermont. Finally, we left even the trees behind for the black rock and lava of the summit.

I remember that it was freezing cold as, wrapped in blankets, the reassembled family peered over into the black lava and red sand of the crater. Then, through clouds of glorious pink and rose and gold and russet, the fiery ball of the sun sank down to touch the ocean. As the flaming sky glowed and faded, Father Wasner spontaneously began the *Polynesian Sunset Hymn.* Softly, we all joined him in this evening prayer in the tongue of the native islands. . . .

The days that followed in Maui were very busy, with singing at different schools in the mornings, programs at the radio station in the afternoons, and concerts at night.

One morning we were driven from our hotel in Wailuku over a beautiful scenic drive to Lahaina, one of the oldest settlements. We caught only a glimpse of the coral stone courthouse and the old mission church, as we passed rapidly on to the Lahaina Luna High School, the oldest school west of the Rocky Mountains. There the whole student body was assembled and waiting in an open hall, where they received us with grace, and kindness, and natural dignity that was most impressive. When we had sung for them, they in turn, with one of the students conducting, sang their school songs.

Afterwards, we learned from the principal that the majority of his pupils were Buddhists, with some Mohammedans, and a few believers in the old Hawaiian faith, but hardly any Christians.

For the first time we felt the full impact of being in a missionary country. That same afternoon, at the school of the Maryknoll Sisters, we came out with the burning question:

"What can we do . . . how should we be . . . ?"

Sister Rose's answering smile was a world of patience: "Be good and kind . . . wait and pray."

There it was again—the lesson we had learned in South America, the lesson we had shared with the seminarians of São Leopoldo, Brazil: "There is no better way of bringing God closer to men than kindness. . . ."

After the evening concert in the Wailuku High School, students presented each one of us with a special lei, no two alike.

"Oho," said one of the backstage visitors, peering at mine, "Mother has a *pikake* lei!" Then, seeing my blank expression, she hastened to add, "A woman who receives a pikake lei has a rare power. When she hangs her lei around a man's neck, he is obliged to do anything she wishes."

Some hours later, still wearing my lei, I knelt for a few moments in the chapel of the Maryknoll Sisters. I was so shaken by the events of the past few hours that I could think of nothing else. Suddenly, my eye fell on a beautiful and life-like statue of Saint Joseph—and that gave me an idea. Walking up to him, I hung my pikake lei around his shoulders, saying fervently, "Please, Saint Joseph, I want the grace of Baptism for everyone in Hawaii!"

And now I can hardly wait for the latter day to find out whether or not Saint Joseph is subject to the law of the pikake lei. . . .

"*Maui no ka oe*—There's no spot like Maui." Over and over again during our stay we heard the words, and our final drive to the airport was filled with memories of all the dear people we had met; of black lava and red sand and a sunset; of The Needle, a slender, steeplelike rock thrusting upward into a deep blue sky. "*Maui no ka oe.*"

There was a crowd waiting at the airport; one last *Aloha Oe*—and then we were once more on the way. . . .

HAWAII

The "Big Island," Hawaii, was only half an hour's flight away. It was there that we experienced the deep, strange mystery of the volcanoes when a group of Maryknoll Fathers drove us one morning up to Halemaumau in the high mountains. Small earthquakes, the ranger told us, had occurred that morning and, at one point, Father informed us gaily that we were standing on a live volcano capable of erupting any minute. We nervously watched the steam, which Johannes mistook for a forest fire; and we almost expected to hear distant rumblings or see darting tongues of flame. If a dinosaur had suddenly come round the curve, or Mother Pele, the Polynesian fire goddess, had changed us all into queer rock formations, I could already have been expecting it. I remember Maria's face as, standing at the edge of a deep pit, we read together the sign: "Rim may crumble at any minute. You are here at your own risk."

Two minutes later, out of prudence, we no longer were. We were on the road back, thinking of how hot lava had once run down the mountainside and how, in the days of the eruptions, the fish for miles around had been boiled in the sea. . . .

On the island of Hawaii we first heard legends of Kamehameha, the ancient king of all the Islands—and heard, too, the long, sad story of how Captain Cook's greedy party disillusioned the Polynesians with all their cheating and mistreating.

We saw coffee groves and groves of macademia nuts; and our heads were full of the poetic sound of Mauna Loa and Mauna Kea. The Hawaiians are a poetic people. Their very names, as well as the names of their villages and towns, sound like songs. On the beach, an old Hawaiian lady identified a cave for me as the "Cave of the Two Lovers," and volunteered the story of two who were unable to marry because of political reasons and preferred to drown themselves together so that their spirits might float forever over the waters of the cave, saying fondly, "Aloha. Aloha."

The "Big Island" cast a curious enchantment. . . .

OAHU

As soon as we landed on the airstrip in Honolulu, our spell was broken. There Mr. Oakley announced to us that the Honolulu audience can be difficult and hard to please, and that the big McKinley Auditorium, where our concert was scheduled, had been by no means sold out. The day that followed was filled with anxious interviews and rehearsals, recalling our most nervous moments in Buenos Aires; and, when we found time to think of it, we worried too over whether Bishop Sweeney and the health authorities had really received the letters asking for permission to visit Molokai.

Only after the concert was over and we had all been applauded, embraced and kissed did we begin to relax, and to realize that we were actually surrounded by old friends. Maybelle was there, and Father McDonald, Superintendent of the Catholic Schools, whom we had already met in Maui. And next to me an unknown lady was murmuring, "Do you remember Malcolm? I'm his mother."

"No!" I said, "not really!"

Malcolm . . . Before my mind's eye rose a picture of our living room in Stowe on a hot summer afternoon, with myself looking down in frowning dismay at a rumpled and smudgy twelve-year-old whom we had taken for the summer because his grandmother wanted him to have the experience of working on a farm. In dirty overalls and even dirtier shoes, he was curled up on our red sofa reading *Smoky*.

"Sorry to disturb you, Malcolm," I said frostily—and then told him in a solid little speech just what I thought. He heard me through attentively, and, when I had finished, said in impeccable English:

"I think I understand fairly well what you mean, Madam, though your pronunciation is far from perfect."

I was too astonished to answer. I simply got him off the sofa and back to the strawberries he should have been weeding . . . and now here was his mother telling me that he still referred to the months in Stowe as the happiest summer of his life. . . . The more one travels, the smaller the world seems to become.

Then came the day of great mistakes. One morning the girls and I were sitting on the front porch of our bungalow at the Niumalu Hotel, humming an old folk song. A tall blond gentleman in red bathing trunks and sunglasses stopped to listen, then came over to put both arms on the railing of the porch and listen some more. When we stopped singing, he asked, "Will you sing something else for me?"

"No, I think not." I was cold and lofty.

"Oh," said the stranger. Disappointedly, he removed his arms from our front porch and walked off.

A few moments later the manager of the hotel appeared. "Ladies," he announced, "Mr. John Ford sends his heartfelt apologies. He did not mean to be rude, and he is sorry to have intruded."

John Ford—the producer of *The Fugitive* and *The Quiet Man!* And I had acted like an iceberg. . . .

Just then Lorli and Johannes came back from the pool, where they had been having a morning dip. "Really, Mother, at first it was too funny." Lorli ascended the porch steps. "There was a tall blond man there who asked Johannes a silly question: 'Where did you learn to dive so well?'—so Johannes said, 'In the water, sir!' "

"Did that tall gentleman perhaps wear red bathing trunks and sunglasses?" I asked lamely.

Lorli: "How did you know?"

We held a consultation of despair, after which Father Wasner, volunteering to act as ambassador, disappeared to find Mr. Ford's bungalow. When he returned, after what seemed endless minutes, he brought an invitation from Mr. and Mrs. Ford for that evening. . . . It was a wonderful party. We sang, and Johannes explained where he had learned to dive; then Mr. Ford told story after story of his experiences as a film producer—and we all parted great friends.

We made many other friends on that island of shower

trees and red hibiscus, bougainvillea, and ginger. The Governor invited us to his palace, the Royal Palace of the Kingdom. We made friends with a very Hawaiian-looking lady, Teresa Malani, descended from the last royal family, who told us that she taught music in a local convent school. Father McDonald introduced us to student members of the Newman Club at the University of Hawaii.

The days that followed were very busy with radio rehearsals, concerts, and school visits. There was almost no time to think and reflect, and very little time for conversation other than, "Where do we meet next?" or "Which program comes now?" We drove over the Pali and sang for native seminarians. We saw the spot where Father Damien's congregation had built their first grass-thatched chapel. We ate with chopsticks—and learned to like raw fish. We drank many little cups of wonderfully scented oriental tea. . . .

And then, one glorious morning, came our ride in an outrigger canoe. We were guests of the Outrigger Canoe Club, and Charlie, one of the Hawaiian boys, was to be our captain. Instructed by him, we helped slide the giant boat into the water. Then we climbed in, sat in single file, and with alternating paddles began to follow his command: "One—two—one—two." Charlie set the course directly at a white line of breakers thundering on the horizon. At last we steered parallel to the combers and waited. Then came a big bulge on the horizon.

"That's *ours!*" Charlie cried. "Now paddle for your life. Faster—faster—*faster!*"

The huge wave came up. We felt it under the boat—then a few more desperate paddle strokes, and Charlie shouted, "Let *go!*" Suddenly, we were flying shoreward, soaring on top of the wave like birds, like clouds driven by the wind, while the spray hit our faces and we could have shouted for joy. . . . The huge wave carried us nearly up the beach. Then the canoe was still.

"Want to go again?" said our captain. *Yes*, we did. But that was our undoing. Again, we paddled through the white whiskers. Again, we lay in wait for "our" wave; again, we saw the solid wall of water move towards us and put every ounce of strength into the last quick paddle strokes— But all at once we were struggling in the water with a great white wall closing over us. . . .

"Abandon ship!" Charlie called out. "Swim away!" He was afraid the canoe might shoot out suddenly. As our heads came above water again, my heart stood still—Father Wasner!

As fast as I could, I swam to tell Charlie: "Father isn't a swimmer." Our captain rose to the emergency. Quietly, he called out, "Father, please come over here, I need you," and, stretching out his arm, he helped Father to find his footing on the rough coral beside him. Next Werner, Lorli, and Johannes were asked to push down on one end of the canoe, while Charlie and Father lifted the other end to rid it of water. Then Johannes was boosted in to bail.

All of this happened much faster than it can be told, and Father Wasner behaved absolutely heroically. Back on terra firma, he and Charlie were the heroes of the day, but afterwards Father left all the surf-boards to us and went firmly off to the terrace of the Outrigger Club to watch all further water sports from dry land. . . .

We tried the surf-boards. After I had seen all my children soaring by, after I had tried it dozens of times myself—always falling hopelessly into the water like a dead fish—Charlie noticed me.

"Come, Mama," he called consolingly. "Now it's our turn. I show you."

"I can't do it, Charlie," I pleaded.

"Oh, but Mama," he said reproachfully. Then, sitting astride his own board, he called out with the voice of a barker at a county fair: "Everybody quiet! This is Mama's wave. Now, Mama, come *on!*"

Everybody stood back. Everybody watched. There came that hateful wave, a dark bulge on the horizon, swiftly approaching, threatening, coming on—and there it was.

"*Now*, Mama! Faster—faster—faster! Get up! Get up! Get . . . *up!*"

Somehow, Mama got up—and soared in. It was glorious, it

was wonderful, it was a triumph—then I, too, retired to join Father Wasner on the terrace of the Outrigger Club. . . .

Not long afterwards we went around to the different mission stations trying, as much as time permitted, to visit them, to sing for them, to learn from them. We went to the Maryknoll houses, to the Sisters of the Sacred Heart, to the Franciscan Sisters at Moana on the outskirts of the town, to the Sisters of Saint Joseph and the Sisters of Notre Dame in the shadow of Diamond Head. . . .

One day, too, Father McDonald arranged a trip through Pearl Harbor. As we boarded the motor boat, I kept repeating to myself, "This is Pearl Harbor—this *is* Pearl Harbor," remembering how I had been called off the stage during a concert in Lynn, Massachusetts, on December seventh, 1941, while the local manager told me I should announce something to the audience: The United States was at war with Japan.

Our boat slowed down beside the hull of the *Arizona*, while we watched the American flag waving in the wind over what had once been a proud battleship—and now was a national monument to the thousand missing sailors. For a few moments the tourist group, of which we were a part, stood in silence; then we sang *My Country 'Tis of Thee*. The officer-in-charge saluted and stood at attention.

Two days later, in the quiet water of the beach at Honolulu, I met a little seamstress from Santa Monica who told me that her only son, aged nineteen, had been killed on Pearl Harbor Day and was buried in Punch Bowl Cemetery. Her husband had since died, and every once in a while, she told me, she would hire out on a boat going to Hawaii—"as stewardess, as charwoman, anything"—so long as it took her to Honolulu. "Here I live cheaply with the natives," she said, "and every day I climb up Punch Bowl to sit with my boy."

> Long may our land be bright,
> With Freedom's holy light . . .

Then, at last, came the long-awaited morning when Bishop

Sweeney graciously received us, and approved our plan to
visit the mission stations on Molokai. Permission from the
health department had been granted; the Bishop had written
about our coming to Father Logan, present-day successor to
Father Damien; and two little private airplanes had been
hired, small enough to come down on the Kalaupapa landing
strip. (His Excellency even added that there were two old
lay brothers in a hospital in Honolulu who remembered
Brother Dutton and had worked with him. At that, Father
McDonough lit up like an electric light bulb, and simply
disappeared.)

As for the rest of us—once again we were eager to go, but
we could not bear to leave. With gladness and sadness, we
made the final plans for departure from Oahu, and the visit
to Molokai. . . .

For the last night, we had been invited to a party at the
house of our "little music teacher," Teresa Malani. Somewhat reluctantly, imagining what we thought must be her
two rooms and kitchenette, we set off at the appointed hour
with friends of hers who had called for us.

But, instead of driving into the heart of the town, the cars
turned towards the residential district, climbed a winding
road through the short tropical twilight, then stopped a little
to one side. We were told to follow our guides through a
shadowy grove: suddenly, we were on a broad lawn circled by
trees and lighted by burning torches. Before us, a long flight
of steps led up to the wide *lanai*, or porch, of a shadowy house.
As we solemnly ascended the stair, a Hawaiian lady in black
evening *holoku* stood on the top step, chanting an ancient
blessing in the native tongue. Behind her on the lanai appeared Teresa, with her husband and son, and what might
have been a gathering at the court of Queen Liliuokalani—
the gentlemen in cloaks of tiny feathers adorned with feath-
ered patterns of red, the ladies in holokus and feather leis.
All were in bare feet, and greeted us with the ceremonial
bow and embrace. Next, we were escorted to a long table set
with ti-leaves and heaped with a staggering profusion of food
of every description: fish, poi, chicken, and vegetables—all

served in coconut shells, to be eaten with the fingers. We did ample justice to the meal, while servers constantly urged us to eat more and "give to the house the honor of appetite." From the garden came the soft twang of guitar and ukulele strings; and, from time to time, the black-clad lady rose to chant a fresh blessing.

For a moment, when Teresa asked us to say an Austrian grace, we returned to our own world and the familiar *Gesegnete Mahlzeit*; then, once again, we found ourselves back in the magic garden where, standing at the foot of the long flight of steps, was a beautiful young girl clothed in a skirt made of ti-leaves, with hibiscus flowers in her dark, flowing hair. "My niece, Leilani," explained Teresa.

Once more we felt ourselves to be in the old Hawaii as Leilani danced, offering the poetry of motion to God in Heaven. Beauty of body and beauty of natural surroundings seemed to become one. Song and music and gesture blended with the eternal rhythm of the sea, whose rolling breakers could be heard in the distance, and with the abiding rhythm of human hearts. First, Leilani danced alone; then little children joined her, like flowers strewn on the waves and swaying gently in the surf. When, finally, she ended—her head gently bent over her knees, both arms outstretched—we could not bear for the evening, or for our stay, to be over.

We could not know then that a year's time would bring us back to Hawaii for a second tour; or that, in Hana-Maui, an audience of only Hawaiians would listen spellbound to the deep pianissimo of the *Tenebrae Factae Sunt*. . . .

All that was still to come, as we sat in Teresa's enchanted garden, clinging fast to our farewell moments, and listening as she spoke to us the timeless incantation:

"Olaka, give grace to the feet and to the bracelets and to the anklets; to each one give gesture and voice. Olaka, make beautiful the lei. Inspire the dancers who stand before the assembly."

As the torches burned down, the old Hawaiians seemed to have forgotten that there were haoles from a faraway country sitting with them on the lanai. They kept reminding one

another, with this story and that, of old times. Gently, our
farewell *Aloha Oe* seemed to take them back to windswept
beaches where the white surf breaks on jet-black sand, where
the ancient hulas first came from the sea—the sea which, for
countless centuries, had evoked for them the haunting refrain,
"Haina ia mai ana kapuana—Let there be an echo of our song."

19

Molokai

So, at long last, our wheels left the ground; and our plane headed for Molokai, the grim heap of black rock that Robert Louis Stevenson had once called "a pitiful place to visit and hell to dwell in."

In those early days before Father Damien, it must have been hell—no hospital, no doctor, no priest; no food, no clothing, no houses; with each fresh shipment of lepers being met on the shore by hundreds of hostile "residents" who pushed the unhappy newcomers back into the water in an attempt to keep themselves from starvation.

We knew that Father Damien's coming had changed all that; that he had stormed the government with repeated appeals for building materials, water-pipes, and financial aid; that, with his own hands, he himself had carpentered over a thousand coffins to bury his parishioners and had slept for many weeks with the living on the bare ground. We knew that every day he had faithfully dressed their wounds, even after that historic morning when his Sunday sermon, ". . . and we lepers . . ." told his parishoners that he, too, had contracted the disease. We knew that Brother Joseph Dutton's work had effected even better conditions in the settlement; but, just the same, as we actually flew over the precipice, the black rocks and jagged coastline looked most unfriendly.

With mixed feelings—and, in some way, the sensation of flying directly into Uncle Craig's postcard collection—we dropped steadily down, past the sixteen hundred feet of

gloomy rock, to the "flat reef," Kalaupapa, the tiny triangle
of the leper settlement. We were somewhat apprehensive.
With all our travels, our only encounter with lepers had been
through the Gospels, in the pleading entreaty of the poorest
of the poor: "Lord, if Thou wilt, Thou canst make us clean."
And in the compassionate answer:

"I will. Be thou made clean."

Now we were to meet them face to face. My heart beat
wildly as we crossed the narrow landing strip towards Father
Logan and his group; and, as we greeted Father, each one of
us made a great effort not to look too closely, not to give an
impression of curiosity; yet, even with the greatest custody of
the eyes, we could not help noticing that in the group of lepers
here and there a nose was missing, or an ear, or part of another feature. The sight drew from us such a great wave of
compassion that our one desire was to show that it did not
matter a bit, that we really loved them all the more. With
outstretched hands I went forward, completely forgetting the
instructions I had received: don't touch the patients; don't
touch anything they may have touched.

What happened next pierced our hearts. The whole row
of people took a few steps back. Arms and hands all vanished
behind their backs; and, though the poor featureless faces
smiled at us, their whole bearing signaled, "We are the un-
touchables."

Mercifully, Father Logan took over. We were speeded into
waiting cars, with our first destination to be, of course,
Brother Dutton's grave in the cemetery of Kalawao, three
miles away. The narrow dirt road took us past many graves—
Buddhist, Catholic, and Protestant—until, at last, after so
many weeks of waiting, we found ourselves standing in a little
church graveyard close under that dark, perpendicular wall
that had always so impressed us in the pictures.

Father Damien had built the church with his own hands.
Brother Dutton's grave, close at hand was marked only with
a simple cross and an inscription: "Joseph Dutton. Born April
27, 1843." Gently, Johannes placed our Mount Mansfield
pine wreath at the foot of the cross. With Father McDonough
leading, each one of us added a lei to the grave and whis-

pered, "*Aloha*, Brother Joseph Dutton. Greetings from Stowe, Vermont."

Then we began to sing. How often have I felt with deepest gratitude this greatest glory of our life as a singing family: that, whenever words failed to say what was taking place in our hearts, we could always express it in music. We sang, and sang, and sang—our whole New England repertoire—until, finally, leaving, we sang a *Te Deum*, too, for Father Damien by the spot where once his grave had been before he was taken back to Belgium.

As Father Logan drove us back across the peninsula, we were impressed to see many attractive little houses, each one surrounded by a beautiful garden with flowering trees and bushes, each little lanai covered with brightly blooming flowers. "Those belong to the patients," Father explained, and went on to tell us that these pretty, comfortable cottages with their lava-stone walls are privately owned. The Territorial Government, through the board of health, has done everything within its power to provide for the comfort and accommodation of these people. Later, when we visited the houses themselves, we saw very nice furniture, musical instruments, books, radios and record players. In the kitchens were modern ranges and, in many a yard, we found the owner's horse, cattle, pigs, or chickens.

During the drive Father patiently answered all our questions and told us of the *kokua*, or helper, system. If a married man goes to Molokai as a leper, his wife is permitted to accompany him, live with him, and help him—or vice versa. If, in addition to housework, such a kokua wants to work for the government, he or she receives pay. All lepers working in and around the settlement receive daily pay as well. There are government stores where all varieties of provisions and equipment are sold at cost. There are machine shops and carpenter shops. There is an electricity plant, an ice plant, storehouses, and a butcher shop. . . .

I cannot say exactly what we had expected, but it certainly was not that. The gloom and the touch of fright which, in our thinking, we had always associated with Molokai, vanished like a lifting fog. . . .

"And now the Sisters are waiting," Father said suddenly, pulling his car to a stop in front of a low, comfortable little house, half-hidden in the trees and flowers of the hospital grounds. Three nuns, dressed in white, were standing on the porch to greet us; and, as Father introduced Sister Hermine, the Superior of the Sisters of Saint Francis, I realized that we had all met before in their convent in Syracuse, New York.

We had a fine reunion over lunch, while the Sisters patiently relived for us the story of their Mother Marianne's first coming to the island thirty years before with five others, and of her firm and reassuring prophecy: "No one of our Sisters will ever contract the disease."

To this day, not one has; but the one condition specified by Mother Marianne, along with her prophecy, was scrupulous cleanliness. After lunch, Sister Hermine showed us through the spacious, airy hospital, explaining, "The hospital is scrubbed every day, and everyone dealing with the patients washes her hands immediately afterwards."

I noticed that she drew us past several closed doors—"the worst cases"—and later, when we were alone together for a few minutes, I pleaded with Sister for permission to be allowed to visit some of them. In her great kindness, she let me, and to the very end of my days I shall be grateful.

We called first on Lahale (Hawaiian for Rachael). She was sitting on her bed dangling what had once been her legs. "Lahale," said Sister, "here is the mother of the singing family, come to visit you." At that, Lahale lit up and burst into a torrent of questions. How was Rupert, and had Johannes come along with us? She had read *The Story of the Trapp Family Singers* and was so sorry that I had lost my husband. . . . Obviously it did not dawn on her that she had any reason for complaining herself, but she was all interest in the Trapp Family and looking forward, oh so much, to their evening concert. . . .

Next, we called on Lapaki (Lawrence). Sister had to tell me that he was only in his late thirties. I could not otherwise have known from the little shriveled face with no eyes or nose—or from the fingerless hands. But when Sister made the introductions, Lapaki's little faceless mouth broke into a broad smile and he asked one enthusiastic question after another. I made a great effort to be casual in all my answers.

So I was taken from room to room, through a living sermon. These people were cheerful and happy, completely resigned to God's Will, so interested in others and forgetful of their own poor selves. . . . As we walked down the steps of the hospital, I wanted to say to Sister, "God reward you for having permitted me to come in such close contact with true holiness," but I could only press her hand.

Supper that night was with Father Logan in the rectory, and the concert that followed was given in the amusement hall—a large center of recreation built not far from the water's edge. Long before the appointed time, the hall was full; and Father said with a smile, peering out at his flock, "I guess no one who can be out of bed is missing tonight."

All I can say about that particular concert is that we put our whole hearts into it, as we had never done before. I remember that, fired by the general enthusiasm of our audience, we went on, and on, and on, till Father Logan came on the stage to say we had been singing for nearly three hours and it was time to stop. Then, knowing his children, he turned to the audience to ask, "Wouldn't *you* like to sing something for our friends?"

This suggestion was greeted with a shout of approval, so the Trapp Family sat down on the stage, and our audience rose. For another half hour they stood there before us, singing. Some of the voices were merely hoarse whispers—Father explained afterwards that the disease, even in its early stages, can affect the vocal cords—but the singing was flawless in rhythm and tone.

"They like you," Father whispered. "Usually they are very shy and retiring, but they know that you are not afraid of them—and truly, you are seeing them at their best."

We spent that night with the Sisters. For a long, long time I lay awake, with my thoughts wandering from Brother Dutton to Father Damien and Mother Marianne; to the heroic suffering and selflessness of Lahale and Lapaki; then to the concert we had been privileged to hear. In the back of my mind, an idea clung: *could* group singing be brought to these people as a permanent pleasure? Would someone be ready and willing to work with them?

I let the question go for a while the next morning, as we followed Father Logan into the Church of Kalaupapa for the Mass of the day. It happened to be the Monday of the Third Week in Lent and, with great emotion, we all read the Epistle of the day: the story of Naaman of Syria, "a valiant man and rich, but a leper," who went to the land of the Jews and "was made clean."

That night there came a sudden sound of instruments—outside a whole orchestra had assembled to serenade us. True, there were some hands with no fingers; the trumpeter was in a wheel-chair, and the drummer had no lips, but the music served only to deepen the peace and joy we had felt in our two days with these serene souls. "Till tomorrow," we said, thanking them and wishing them goodnight.

When the next day came, and we hurried for the airport, it was pouring rain. "Please don't be disappointed," Father Logan said apologetically. "No one will be at the landing field to wave you off. The patients are very much affected by wet weather. It hurts them so much physically that they must simply stay indoors until the sun comes out again. I just want you to understand."

We understood, of course. Someone had told us that in the Islands rain is "liquid sunshine." . . . But at the air-port, dripping and smiling, we found the whole settlement, patiently waiting in the drenching downpour.

There were tears, and there were presents: bouquets and leis for each one of us, plus a beautifully carved little whale-bone cross made by one of the men. The rain splashed in sounding drops around us as we all sang together, "*Aloha Oe* —Until we meet again." At the last minute Sister Hermine said simply, "You may accept all the gifts. They were fumigated early this morning."

Then our wheels left the airstrip and we rose and circled, looking down once again over the steep black wall of Molo-kai's pali, knowing that we were leaving behind lifelong friends—in the golden shadow of the liquid sunshine.

20

Wheels at Home

The years 1953 and 1954 brought some of the most solemn and meaningful moments of our life together as a family. We were seldom home—in fact, we seemed to be traveling more than ever; and our spring tour of 1953 even took us back to Hawaii for two weeks of concerts—but when we *were* at home there were many days of special rejoicing.

Early in that year Rupert's little Elizabeth was born, joining brother Georgie and sister Monique. Rupert's wife, Henriette, had had a severe bout with polio only a few years before, so we were holding our breath with anxiety; and the news that all had gone well was good news indeed. Then on February sixteenth came Werner and Erika's Bernhard, baptized a week later in the chapel at Cor Unum. (The following year, when their little Maria Elizabeth was born, I realized that I had become a grandmother for the twelfth time!)

1954 brought the celebration of two beautiful family feasts: for Monsignor Wasner and for Lorli. On Easter Monday we celebrated the twenty-fifth anniversary of our Monsignor's ordination to the priesthood. Old friends came flocking to Cor Unum for the occasion, and he sang his Jubilee Mass with Father Christopher Huntington as sub-deacon and Father Paul Taggart preaching the sermon. We presented Monsignor Wasner with a rare fifteenth-century chalice; a relic of the True Cross in an ancient reliquary; and a white chasuble made and embroidered by different members of the family. Werner had contributed the gold letters: "I.H.S." As a special joy we were able to tell him that many loving friends all over the world had united to send him a purse which would enable him to visit his home in Austria and to celebrate a Jubilee Mass at the altar where he had celebrated his first.

During lunch and the speeches that followed, our hearts were filled with deep thanksgiving. Of the twenty-five years of his priesthood, Father Wasner had spent nineteen with us—as priest, friend, conductor, and Rock of Gibraltar. He had taught us to be both the Trapp Family Singers and Cor Unum—a community of people with one heart and one mind. His great patron, Saint Francis de Sales, said once that a single soul is diocese enough for a bishop, but our Monsignor's parish today includes a world of souls—literally some hundreds of thousands, who have received a message of God through listening to his music or through knowing him personally.

On Trinity Sunday, June thirteenth, came the wedding of our Lorli and Hugh Campbell. They had known each other since Hugh's first days as a Music-Camper, and he had visited us in Salzburg in 1950. The engagement had been solemnized in January and had made us all very happy, though I found it hard to believe that my little Lorli, who only yesterday, it seemed, had been racing around with her braids flying, was really old enough to marry. Announcements had been sent to friends at home and abroad. Though we all offered to help her, Lorli had preferred to address every one of the nine hundred and fifty envelopes herself.

In May, when the time came to send out invitations, I had quite a surprise. "I'm only inviting close relatives and friends," Lorli said—and handed me a list of one hundred and ten names. Hedwig took one look at the length of this and departed—to check blankets and find more beds!

The last weeks before a wedding are bitter-sweet. White brocade was selected and transformed into a patrician wedding garment of old Austria. My own bridal veil was made ready to be handed on to my daughter. We were all looking

forward to the great day, but with a "for the last time" feeling
that made for a special tenderness.

On Tuesday, June seventh, Hugh arrived. Family and
friends took care of last-minute details, while Lorli, Hugh,
and I spent much time in serious discussion of the spiritual
meaning of family life. We also talked about what love is—
and what it is not. On Friday Lorli and Hugh spent a Day of
Recollection with Monsignor Wasner, who spoke to them of
the mysteries of the great Sacrament of Matrimony.

Then suddenly it was Saturday and the guests had begun
to arrive: Hugh's mother and family from Rhode Island;
Rupert and Henriette, with little George and Monique; then
many friends of Cor Unum in a steady stream of traffic coming over the hill.

At six o'clock we escorted our one hundred and ten relatives and friends to the big meadow that lies next to our farm
and overlooks the Nebraska Valley. The weather forecast had
indicated showers for the late afternoon and evening, and
many an anxious look was sent up to the cloudy sky, but not
a drop fell. Around the great open fireplace, our friends from
Canada had gathered—Pierre, Jean, and Jacques, to don white
aprons and produce delicious barbecued chicken, while Agathe and Hedwig served up the rest of the picnic supper.

When the last bite was gone and the last plate had been
removed, I drove the jeep into the meadow—a "musical" jeep,
carrying Werner with his clarinet and Maria with her accordion. As this was Lorli's last evening at home, she was to
select all her favorite folk dances; so for a time everyone
joined in, while the music sounded merrily out across the
meadow and down into the valley.

Then just at sunset, Father Wasner and Louella Apiki sang
Ke Kali Ne Au. We had come to know Louella and her high,
birdlike voice during our second trip to Hawaii. Father Mc-
Donald, Superintendent of Schools, had asked her to sing for
us. When we learned that her mother was in the leper colony
on Molokai and that she had no real home, we had brought
her back with us to Stowe—and now, on this wedding evening,
she and Monsignor Wasner sang together the song that had

introduced her to us, *Ke Kali Ne Au*, the old Hawaiian wedding song, in which the man's voice begins, the girl's replies, and the two voices then blend into one.

After that, through the falling dark, we sang together for our guests, with Lorli for the last time as our leading soprano. As we finished, the night was really upon us, and the last glowing coals of the barbecue fire had burned out. Everyone present knelt in the meadow for Monsignor Wasner's evening blessing, and we sang the Brahms *Lullaby* with a feeling of deep peace and unity.

For the next day, pouring rain had been predicted. The early morning sky was cloudy, and a few drops fell, but not enough to dampen the spirits of the day. Besides, we had already learned in Hawaii that rain is liquid sunshine. . . .

There was a moment of panic at half-past nine—no one could find the bride. She finally appeared rosily from the cellar, where she had been making up bouquets for her sisters, who were to be her bridesmaids. Then she came to my room, and, according to the old custom, the mother dressed the bride. It was a touching moment when my child knelt before me in her white dress and veil, and I fastened on her head the wreath of white flowers, symbol of virginity, saying:

"I have helped you to preserve it that you may hand it untarnished to the husband God has chosen for you." I gave her the bouquet of white roses that Hugh had sent, and we went downstairs.

The chapel in the house would have been far too small, so Lorli was married in the Saint Cecilia Chapel of the Music Camp, down at the foot of the hill. As the wheels of our car came to a stop, we could see a host of friends waiting outside to form a procession. There were no spectators for this wedding. Everyone present was part of the procession, with the groom first, escorting the mother of the bride.

In my home, the Zillertal in Tyrol, it is customary for the pastor to come to the house of the bride and solemnly lead her to the church. We were doubly grateful now to have Monsignor Wasner follow this beautiful tradition and so to replace Lorli's father, who could not be in person with his child.

Hugh's brother, Wally, was best man; and last of all came Rupert's little George and Werner's young Barbara carrying the bride's long veil.

Inside the chapel a fragrant arch of flowers and garlands had been erected in the center aisle over the seats of the bride and groom. After Monsignor Wasner had vested for the Solemn High Mass, he approached the young couple and solemnly addressed them:

"Henceforth you will belong entirely to one another. You will be one in mind, one in heart, one in affections. Whatever sacrifices you may be required to make to preserve this common life, always make them generously. Sacrifice is usually difficult and irksome. Only love can make it easy, and perfect love can make it a joy. We are willing to give in proportion as we love; and when love is perfect, the sacrifice is complete."

At the end of the wedding ceremony, the entire congregation sang an eighteenth-century *Alleluia* by Philip Hayes. Then Holy Mass followed. Father Russell Woollen, one of our oldest friends, conducted the music throughout: Monsignor Wasner's *Missa Brevis*; Palestrina's *O Bone Jesu* at the Offertory; and at the end, with everyone joining in, *Holy God We Praise Thy Name*.

Then we all—with this time the two mothers walking together—followed Mr. and Mrs. Hugh Campbell out of the chapel. I glanced at Lorli and was deeply moved by her expression of serenity and radiant happiness.

The wedding breakfast was served back up at the farm, at a great, horseshoe-shaped banquet table set up the night before in the large living room of the guest wing. When the right moment came, Lorli and Hugh cut the huge wedding cake standing in front of them—a white masterpiece made from an old Austrian recipe and decorated by Illi with alpine flowers made of sugar.

Then came the toasts: a toast to the bride, proposed by Monsignor Wasner; a toast to the two mothers, proposed by Hugh's brother, Wally. Hugh rose to toast the two fathers who had gone ahead. My toast, the last one, was "to all friends present and afar."

We had not noticed how time was flying. It was almost two o'clock. As Lorli and Hugh were to drive to New York that same day, it was high time for them to change. Their car was already packed with bicycles, sleeping-bags, and all the other equipment necessary for a summer of hiking and camping in Europe. One last goodbye to them upstairs, then I joined the others at the front door. They were "decorating" the car and waiting for the young couple. But while friends and musicians waited expectantly in front, Lorli and Hugh slipped out the back door, around the side of the house—and in five seconds they were in the car and gone, with a fine cloud of dust rising behind their disappearing wheels. . . .

The clarinet and accordion struck up a merry dance, and soon all the guests standing in front of the house had joined in. For a moment I stood by myself on the porch looking down the empty road, and my thoughts went back—as they had been going back all day—to the Gospel text for the preceding Sunday: "If you loved Me, you would be glad that I go."

"How wonderful it will be in Heaven," I thought to myself, "with *no more farewells*."

Then I went down to join the dancing.

21

New Zealand:
"Never Mind the Weather"

Our last foreign tour was to New Zealand and Australia. This time there were eleven to be seen off at the airport by Freddy Schang: Monsignor Wasner, Agathe, Maria, Hedwig, Werner, Johannes, and myself—plus four young friends who had come to join our singing family: Barbara Stechow, Annette Brophy, Pietro LaManna, and Alvaro Villa. Barbara had first come to Stowe as a Music-Camper from Oberlin, Ohio, and played both recorder and flute. Alvaro had heard us sing in Medillin, Colombia, and had simply "dropped in" at Cor Unum, guitar in hand, on a busy day in the midst of the Christmas season. So we had borrowed both of them: Barbara's manifold artistry, Alvaro's mellow Spanish voice—and, of course, the guitar. Pietro—after the first day we were calling him Peter— was a fine tenor, an acquaintance of the Spaar sisters; and Annette a birdlike high soprano, who had come to us from Ogden, Utah, via the Julliard School.

Farewells were not easy on that spring day in 1955, especially for Werner and Erika, whose fifth child, Toby, was born a few hours before the departure. Besides, we had never been away from home for seven months without a break, and the details of our tour, as we had received them from the overseas manager, seemed a little vague. Freddy Schang's last words, as we boarded the plane, were: "I hope you won't regret this"—and we knew that he was remembering a certain urgent telephone call from Paris. . . .

We reached Honolulu, stopped, then went on to Canton

Island. Somewhere, before or after, we crossed the International Date Line—and Lorli's birthday, May twelfth, disappeared completely from our calendar. It was good to know that Lorli herself was celebrating the day in a less irregular hemisphere—with Hugh and baby Elizabeth, born two months before.

Fiji—and the Nandi airport. It was warm. During the short stop we caught a glimpse of dark-skinned, barefoot policemen in funny petticoats, with black hair standing out around each head like a scrubby halo. . . .

Then, at last, at half-past five in the evening, after we had been thirty-six hours in the air, our plane wheeled to a stop on the landing field at Auckland, New Zealand. It was no longer warm. In the southern hemisphere, May corresponds to November as far as weather is concerned. We stepped off the plane into a cold, drenching downpour, with the chill of winter in the air. . . .

We had only recently emerged from a deep, snowed-in New England winter and we were hungry for sunshine and warmth. Ten minutes in Auckland, and we knew that we would continue to be hungry for some time. The New Zealand management had answered our advance questions on weather with the reassurance that our regular New York clothing would be just right, but it took us no time at all to realize that this meant "out-of-doors, of course."

Indoors, the only average source of warmth we were to find in any house was the old-fashioned fireplace; though rare progressives here and there would add an electric heater consisting of a single little glowworm of red-hot wire. Hotels were sometimes "heated"—by a two-foot section of pipe vaguely lukewarm to the touch. Occasionally, one might huddle over a "roaring gas jet" and I can tell of doors and windows left open all day because "when the sun shines, it is warmer outside."

Everywhere we went, the rain poured down, or dripped down, or drizzled down, and the cold grew more and more bitter. Rubbing the hands is a national winter sport in New

Zealand. So is blowing on the fingers. We learned to do both.

"But, my dear," said one of the nuns at the convent where we stayed in Auckland, "it is really a hot day for this season of the year." I know she meant it. In the chapel all the windows—eleven on each side—were wide open, and chilly gusts blew through the curtains. Quietly, I went from one to another, closing them—and, just as quietly, came one of the Sisters close behind me, reopening each one "to let the warm air in."

One night I heaped every possible blanket on top of me, having already arranged myself on an "upper berth" of two mattresses besides. At first, I indignantly declined anything so lowly as a hot-water bottle—after all, I'm no baby. Later, when asked, I was reduced to answering meekly, "Could I please have two?" Hot-water bottles in New Zealand come in all colors and shapes—as dolls, or birds, or Easter bunnies. When we discovered, as we soon did, that concert halls and theatres were, for the most part, unheated, and that night after night our audiences snugly wrapped woolen blankets over their thick fur coats, we wished fervently that hot-water bottles could be put on the market in the shape of violins or cellos, such as a concert artist might, with some dignity, have with him on the stage.

"Never mind the weather," we said at Greymouth. Was it at the Greymouth concert that Hedwig ingeniously slipped hot-water bottles under the tablecloth where the recorders were, to keep them in pitch until they were used? I remember, at least, that that particular stage was the coldest and windiest we had ever encountered, and so drafty that the curtain swayed all through the performance. Even the hot tea someone brought us during the intermission did not seem to help. The recorders worked beautifully, but we did not; and, at last, as we looked down at our wrapped-and-furred listeners, we could stand it no longer. We came on in jackets. I think I never before cried from the cold.

Near Wellington—at Lower Hutt—we visited the Cenacle nuns, among them two dear friends whom we had known years before in New York. The wind that day was absolutely unbearable, and the temperature was well below freezing.

"Mother," we said, blowing fashionably on our fingers, "how do you stand the weather?"

"I never mind the weather," Mother answered with an air of sub-zero detachment. "When it's really cold—I put on another layer." Then, seeing our startled sidelong glance at the flowing folds of her religious habit, she added quickly, "Underneath, of course."

So the next day we all went shopping furiously. It might be said that, from then on, we lived out our stay in New Zealand in a long succession of one-layer, two-layer, and three-layer days.

The New Zealand management, Kerridge-Odeon, was brisk, efficient and capable. On our first visit to Mr. Kerridge's office, the day after we reached Auckland, we were given a tour manager and handed a complete itinerary, à la Schang, with dates, halls, times, etc.—the whole thing neatly typed in eleven copies, one for each. As we read down the page, however, a profound silence settled over the group. We were to sing, all in all, with matinees and evening concerts, at least ten times a week. . . .

We managed! But at the start, at least, things did not really go too well. Ten concerts a week proved almost more than human vocal cords could endure—ten concerts in addition to innumerable High Masses, Benedictions, visits to hospitals, visits to orphanages.

We learned, too, that Auckland is not the right place to begin. We felt with the old Vermonter who said, "If I was goin' there, I wouldn't start from here." There had been a series of concerts that fall, the public was exhausted, the children were on vacation. Publicity, itself, seemed rather casually handled by our efficient management. More than once, our first concert in a town was used to advertise the second; and in Wellington, the capital, it took us nearly a week to overcome the fact that advance notices had called us a "yodel group." More than once, too, poor Agathe removed our concert clothes from the suitcases only to find that there was no way to connect her electric iron; whereupon, we all appeared onstage looking a little—to quote Alvaro—"as though we had come in suitcases ourselves."

Whatever the reasons, it meant that once more we went through the depressing experience of singing to half-empty or half-filled houses; and, at one point, I began secret investigations about the cost of a phone call from New Zealand to Columbia Concerts in New York.

Then, gradually, things became better established. The *Echo Song* proved just as popular "down under" as it had "on top." Night after night, stirring applause greeted Father Wasner's arrangement of the *Hawaiian Wedding Song*. At last, in Christchurch, we had the unique experience of singing evening after evening, for a whole week, to full houses, while for a whole week, morning after morning, newspaper reports were appreciative, understanding, and increasingly enthusiastic; and, in between, we ourselves came to know and love the sensitive musicianship of Foster Browne, choir master of the famous boys' choir in the Anglican Cathedral. He had suggested our visit.

So we sang on, from one town to the next. One morning in—where was it?—I received a short note: "I am the chef in your hotel. I heard you sing last night. My wife is dying of cancer at the hospital. For weeks she planned to go to your concert, but now she is too sick. Do you think you could sing for her?"

We stopped at the hospital and sang for her—on a big sunporch where all the patients who could walk or be wheeled had assembled. Next to her stood our chef, a ruddy-faced man beaming with joy. "I know I won't get well," the invalid whispered to me. "I just want to keep myself as long as possible for my dear husband." Two months later, a letter from her nurse told us that he had died first—suddenly, of a heart attack—and that his wife had followed him. The nurse thanked us for "their last great joy together."

So, off-stage and on, we went on singing, from one night

to another, until we had sung one hundred and five concerts in all.

Most of the time we spent the nights with local families. Perhaps, because the Vienna Choir Boys had asked to stay in private homes, the manager thought that all Austrians must prefer this type of accommodation. We were very grateful, of course, but more than once the distribution produced some funny situations—as, for instance, when the six "ladies" were escorted to two double beds and two little sofas, while the gentlemen "made themselves at home" in one tiny living room.

One night I was put up in the home of a bachelor and shown to what was obviously his housekeeper's private room. Every two minutes she would burst in with a polite, "Excuse me, if I disturb you," to get something from her wardrobe, her chest of drawers, her night table—until I suddenly realized that, while I stayed in *her* room, she, herself, was trying to manage in the guest room across the hall. To my astonished question as to whether it might not have been easier for her to put me there in the first place, she answered candidly, "But now I can tell my friends that you have slept in my bed!"

The fact that we never learned to sleep two in a bed proved increasingly awkward, especially when it meant struggling for the proper words and phrases with which to convince the daughter of the house that it was not the fact that you did not want to sleep with *her*, but that you *never* could sleep with someone else. . . .

And how many times I was roused from an afternoon nap by the sound of a penetrating whisper outside my door: "Is she *still* sleeping?" It was all so kindly, so generous, that one could only try not to disappoint.

"There are two kinds of hotels," we wrote home to Stowe, "those where the Queen has been, and those where she has not." Peter was particularly impressed by the spots where Her Majesty had preceded us, and liked nothing better than to sign his name somewhere under that strong, sweeping signature, "Elizabeth R." He became a devoted subject, and nothing exasperated him more than a hotel room where pictures of the Queen and her husband were hung facing away from one another. When no one was watching, he would reverse them.

Werner was demonstrative, too; but in another way. New Zealand hotels will not soon forget his booming, early-morning, "Take away that TEA!" (Tea, according to local custom, is brought to one's bedside at seven A.M.) More than one nervous little housemaid went suddenly flying down the hall, away from Werner's door, teacup still in hand.

In Wellington a famous scene occurred when an authoritative maid, not knowing to whom she spoke, woke Werner one morning by tapping him on the shoulder, with the statement:

"It's time for morning tea, sir."

"I don't think so," answered Werner, calm, and sleepy, and confused.

"Oh, but it is, sir."

Suddenly, Werner awoke. I shall quote no more. It is enough to say that the girl disappeared. We never saw her again, with tea or without it.

Actually most of us became devoted to the various "teas": "early morning tea," "morning tea," "afternoon tea," "tea at five," or, in our own case, "tea backstage." In fact, eventually, cold or no cold, we became devoted to New Zealand. We fell in love with the "trifle" and with "tree tomatoes" and "Chinese gooseberries." We learned to speak of mutton as "hogget" or "colonial goose"; we were held spellbound by the kiwis, by the seals and chamois of the Southern Alps; and by the glaciers—pronounced "glassiers."

As time went on, we felt ourselves drawn more and more closely—as Hedwig said, "layer by layer"—to the kindliness we encountered on all sides. Each town or city went to great pains to organize a little reception, where usually some prelate or dignitary gave the welcoming speech; then the "word" was passed to Father Wasner, and passed again to me, until, finally, the comfortable ritual concluded with a little phrase we came to know and expect: "And now, perhaps, we should not let the tea get too cold."

This happened everywhere, in small towns as well as large. (We were also received by the Maoris, but that is a chapter in itself.) Wherever we went, we felt really welcomed, included, not only within the gates of the town, but in the hearts of its citizens. The Mayor and Lady Mayoress of Masterton lit up a miserably cold day with their warm cordiality. The Mayor of Nelson arranged a sight-seeing trip. The Mayor of Wellington, when he realized we were interested, had his state robes brought out, complete with chain and sceptre, and put them on to show us how he had appeared before the Queen. In more than one town there was an orchid corsage for me—which I once, unthinkingly, left for a chapel altar and then quickly had to reclaim so as not to offend the donor that evening at the concert. In Dunedin we heard the bagpipes skirl . . . and so it went, through New Plymouth, Greymouth, Palmerston North: until, from all of them, Johannes chose the Mayor of Dunedin as his favorite because he seemed "almost American."

At night, people waited outside the concert hall until we had packed and changed; then, when we came out, there were always warm handclasps and friendly words, sometimes a "hip, hip, hooray." Once an entire group sang, *Now Is the Hour,* the national song of New Zealand, as we boarded the bus; and, as the cold wheels moved off through the cold night, we answered with the Brahms *Lullaby.*

It is true that we never understood in New Zealand how a nation could seem to enjoy freezing itself through the long winter months, but in the course of our stay we came to think of zero weather as fairly normal, and we developed for all New Zealanders what might be called a one-layer, two-layer —then a three-layer—affection.

22

Haeremai

The Maoris won our hearts completely. "And to think," Maria mused one day, "that one hundred years ago they might have eaten us—even if they'd had tickets to a Trapp Family concert for the following night!"

The Maoris are the natives of New Zealand. They are Polynesian, and in language, features, and grace of bearing very like the Hawaiians, although to us they seemed more hearty and vigorous. (Johannes attributes this sturdiness to the cold climate of New Zealand.) Not so very long ago, some of the Maoris were still cannibals; and even today they continue to maintain their own villages and ancient tribal customs. Age-old legends are deeply interwoven with the history and myths of their race and culture, and their music—for there is no such thing as an unmusical Maori—has handed down the traditions of one generation to another.

Our "first acquaintance" came in Hamilton at an after-concert party, where Amiria Rika, "Mrs. Rice," as we called her, enchanted us with stories of her Maori home in Rotorua —with old tales of Aotearoa, the Land of the White Cloud, and with *Pokare kare ana*, the legendary love song of a Maori prince and princess:

> *Pokare kare ana*
> *Nga waio Rotorua*
> *Khiti atu koe hine*
> *Marino ana e.*

Rotorua waves are stormy,
Rotorua waves are wild,
But where you have passed, my dear one,
All the sea is calm and mild.
Maid of my longing,
Turn now to me,
My heart is yearning,
Beside the sea.

The Maori language is Polynesian, not unlike what we had heard in Hawaii, and, in a very short time we found we could join Amiria for the tune and words of the first verse:

"E hine e—
Hoki mai ra,
Kamate au i
To aroha e—"

The simple refrain sings of a very hopeful longing. We left the party that night humming our first Maori folk song, and Father Wasner went home to work out a choral arrangement. . . .

"Just wait until you come to Rotorua," everyone told us. "There you will really meet the Maoris." So we came to Rotorua—to be disappointed at first. Rotorua has become such a tourist center that even when Rangi, the well-known Maori guide, put her best into showing us the *pa*, or native village, it seemed made-to-order, and we were not really touched. We knew we had not yet met the real Maoris.

That evening we invited Rangi and several of her friends to the concert. Afterwards, when they came backstage, we sensed again, through their excitement, the universal power of the language of music. And then "it" happened: Rangi invited us to her home "to show us something."

We went. The house had been built by her grandfather in a wide-gabled style that reminded us of Austrian farmhouses. Once inside, we were invited to sit on furs on the floor and to be part—at last—of a group of real Maoris. We sang for them, we all sang together; and then they sang for us; old chants, and action songs where the whole body portrays the content of the story sung. Then, finally, we were privileged to witness a Maori dance reserved only for women —the *poi* dance.

A poi in New Zealand is not to be confused with the national dish of Hawaii. As these Maori girls stepped forward, each one carried a pair of balls suspended on long strings. (The poi, itself, is about the size of an orange and was originally made of leaves.) Singing, bending, swaying, the dancers began to twirl the pois—in eights, in reverse curves, in a progression of intricate figures, each more graceful than the last.

The effect on all of us was electric. Father McKenna, the local pastor, had to arrange the next day for native Maori girls to give us poi lessons between a matinee and an evening performance. We learned that there are two different pois: the long and the short. The long poi was formerly reserved for maidens of royal blood, while the short poi was used by anyone. To our chagrin, Werner and Johannes were the first ones to master the intricacies of swinging the patterns—but, as men, they were forever disqualified from performing the dance.

In Hastings we found that the Albert Hotel, hot or cold, had one great asset: waitresses, chambermaids and kitchen personnel were all Maori. In no time the Trapp Family had resumed its poi lessons; and Agathe, Maria, Barbara or Annette could be found unexpectedly on back staircases, in the lounge, in the dining room, or in the corridor—practicing. One needs ample room for the poi dance.

As an "exchange of goods," we invited our poi teachers to a concert—then, afterwards, "it" happened again. Three gentlemen—three elders of the Maori community—presented themselves at the hotel, requesting the "honor" of our presence the next evening at the Pa Kahupatiki where their entire tribe would be ready to receive us. . . .

That evening has gone down in Trapp Family history. Our bus drove us up to the pa where we were met by a young man who guided us to the meeting house: suddenly, we seemed to be transported into one of Georg's famous stories, peopled by native women with flower wreaths and long flowing hair, by gentlemen in loincloths made of native fiber. Our hosts were all dressed in the ancient Maori fashion.

As we entered, an old, old chief—one of the last, I later learned—hobbled forward on his crutch, stretched out his right arm and, in a deep voice shaken with feeling, called out the tribal welcome: *"Haeremai . . . Haeremai . . . Haeremai!"* Chant and songs and poi dances followed—then, finally, the breath-taking war dance of the men, the *haka*.

We have always been folk-dance-minded. We have seen many national dances of many countries; but with the haka we sensed for the first time that a dance can be music, painting, and sculpture all in one. The floor trembled as the dark bodies stamped and whirled through one intricate rhythm-pattern after another; the air shook to the sound of their strident war cries . . . and, all the while, as we watched, an old grandmother was explaining to me in a murmur that in the olden days enemy groups tried to intimidate one another before a battle by dancing the haka, outdoing one another in ferocity and wildness, while on both sides, behind the lines, the women prepared the fire for the kettle. . . .

Word spread fast that the Trapp Family were particularly interested in the Maoris. In Napier we were invited for "morning tea" at an academy for Maori girls conducted by the Sisters of St. Joseph, while Uncle Charles Baldwin, our tour director, arranged for us to visit an Episcopalian academy nearby. (He was always most sympathetic to our interest, but he firmly refused to accompany us.)

Then, in Wellington, Father Wall, the chaplain of the Maoris, invited us to join them for an evening in their meeting house. Remembering our evening in Hastings, we expected a chanted welcome and an aged chieftain calling out "Haeremai." Simple and unsuspecting, we entered the hall. Father Wall motioned Father Wasner to go first, while the rest of us followed close behind. . . . Suddenly, there was an indescribable howl. A huge, grass-skirted Maori charged directly towards Father Wasner, while we watched—speechless with horror. His eyes flashed under his bushy hair. He jumped, groaned, stretched out his tongue, and licked his lips . . . while Father Wall dispassionately made no attempt to save our lives. At that moment, the wild cannibal laid his club at Father Wasner's feet.

"Pick it up," whispered Father Wall.

Father Wasner picked it up.

"This is Ananea," Father Wall gave the introductions calmly.

Ananea's wild face broke into a beaming smile. Meek as a lamb, he followed, while we wobbled on weak knees to our seats in the first row.

The evening began very formally (the "word" was handed round, and round, and round, till it came to rest with Father Wasner and myself) and ended with a stupendous haka led by Ananea. In conclusion, we sang some of our own songs, telling the assembled group that, from now on, we planned to include Maori songs and dances in our program for the benefit of all those who might not otherwise have known of them.

The Maoris looked impressed, but a little incredulous. At the next concert they were present to see if the Trapp Family really meant to keep their word. Meanwhile, Annette, Barbara and Maria had mastered the poi dance—so, after the last encore in English, we began Father Wasner's new arrangement of *Pokare kare ana*. The girls stepped forward and the audience, seeing the pois in their hands, broke out in a riot of applause. . . .

We kept our word. In every concert after Wellington—across Australia and home again—the poi dance came as an encore. At Dunedin, where the last concert was sold out, we had the surprising experience of seeing a red streamer come sailing onto the stage during the poi song. It was followed by another one, yellow; then a blue; then a green. For a moment we were stunned—until we understood, and caught them as they came flying thick and fast, like rockets, from the dark of the audience—and we sang *Now Is the Hour* with the pois and the multi-colored ribbons wound in our fingers, as a new and lovely symbol of the international, inter-racial bond of music.

23

Australia:
"You'll Come A-Waltzing"

·

In Australia we learned that kangaroos travel by taking off in a flying leap. After that, they just keep on jumping, happily hitting the ground here and there at intervals of about twenty feet or more.

So did the Trapp Family bus.

The sturdy little blue vehicle was waiting for us at the Sydney airport, with nice Mr. Jack Neary from the management ready to help us in. In no time at all we went bounding off towards the city.

Sydney is spread out around its various bays and inlets. The outskirts—very up and coming, and industry-minded—suddenly reminded me of the U.S.A. As we crossed the handsome concrete-and-cable bridge spanning the bay, our driver stopped the bus for a solemn and impressive announcement:

"This bridge," he informed us, with a sweeping gesture, "is the greatest engineering accomplishment of our time. It has x-thousand rivets, y-thousand tons of iron, and sixty-five suicides."

He paused for effect, and the bus jumped forward once again.

Most of our Australian travel was by bus, with once in a while a routine train- or plane-flight, for variety. Mr. Neary explained at the start that we were to make an extended stay in the larger cities—Sydney, Melbourne, Brisbane, Adelaide—with short tours organized from each to take us into the back country. The schedule he handed us read something like this:

August 15–26.   Sydney

August 26.   *New South Wales Country Tour*
                Bus Sydney to Maitland (125 miles).
                Concert Maitland. Leave Sydney in
                time to reach Bandgate (113 miles) for
                broadcast interview.

August 27.   Bus. Maitland to Tamworth (158
                miles). Picnic lunch if weather fine.
                Press and radio interview to be fixed on
                arrival. Concert Tamworth.

August 30.   Bus. Tamworth to Armidale (69
                miles).

August 31.   Armidale to Glen Innes.

And so on: Gunnedah . . . Gunnedah to Coolah . . . to
Mudgee . . . to Dubbo . . . to Orange. Then, finally, as
a last entry on the page:

September 10.   Bus. Very early start from Orange to
                Sydney (166 miles). Go directly to air-
                port to catch plane at 2:15 for Bris-
                bane. Essential to arrive Brisbane in
                time for interviews and photos for the
                Sunday papers.

So, once again, in the original sense, we became a "Family
on Wheels," and, as a "Family on Wheels," we "discovered"
Australia. Once again, as long ago in the United States, we
learned to get used to not getting used to things. We never
quite adjusted, for instance, to having the seasons upside-
down. We had frozen through June and July in New Zealand.
Now, on August fifteenth in Sydney—the Feast of the Assumption—it was still cold, but with a faint and hopeful
touch of spring in the air. I soon learned not to retreat rapidly,
making second-alto sounds of distress, if a monster-lizard suddenly appeared beside me in the spring sun of the hotel
garden. By late September, spring was official, and everything

was green. En route between Castlemaine and Maryborough, I noted in my diary: "Beautiful drive through spring apple blossoms and lush green sheep country"; and, in late October, when we reached Adelaide, the weather was really hot and sticky. We all had a good swim, while people around us remarked that already there was a "hint of Christmas" in the air. . . .

Strangely exotic wildlife occasionally surrounded us as we bus-bounded from town to town. Flocks of cockatoos flew up from the trees and fences, changing in their flight from pink to gray as they turned in the sunlight and disappeared in the distance. Bright-colored parrots and parakeets would suddenly shine up in the bushes along the road; and occasionally a lonely kookaburra, or "laughing jackass," settled in a nearby tree, showering the bus with a dose of his oversize laughter. In Sydney, at the zoo, we saw our first kangaroos and wallabies —and that sweetest of all wild animals, the koala bear, a lovely, good-natured, trusting little creature that clings like a baby. As for the flowers—we drove through hills and meadows bright blue with blossoms and will always remember the blue tinsel lilies and the gold of the wattle tree.

At other times we were awed by the very emptiness around us. Closing my eyes now, I can still see the far-stretching valleys between low-rounded, grayish brown hilltops—miles and miles of uninhabited land with here and there a solitary sheep station; and everywhere, from plain to plain and from valley to valley, the stout, twisted trunks and silvery leaves of the gum tree, the eucalyptus.

Without eucalyptus, there could be no Australia. We had hardly been twenty-four hours in Sydney when we were driven out into the bush for a giant-size picnic with the Good Shepherd Sisters in a thick grove of the slippery-trunked, towering trees. Two weeks later, we had hardly left Sydney for our "back-country tour" ("Picnic lunch if weather fine") when, suddenly, the bus pulled off the road in the shadow of some rather scraggly gum trees close by a little brook.

"Not real bush," the driver explained, "but a good spot for lunch." Then, while the girls arranged our picnic and

Johannes and Alvaro tried desperately to scale the slippery tree trunks, we had our first sample of "billy tea."

For this, the driver entered into deep consultation with Mr. Longdon of the management. A "spot" was selected: close to the lazy water of the brook and protected by a little bridge. Next, a fire was built. Then a green stick was suspended over the fire "to keep away the smoke"; and on the stick the two of them hung a large can full of water.

"This is our billy," Mr. Longdon explained.

Maria's voice, mystified, was heard in a whispered undertone, "Who?"

We gathered, indirectly, that the water was in the billy, that the tea would go into the water, and that both would boil together. So they did. Then billy tea was served, steaming, and strong, and fragrant. That picnic was like no other. . . .

Once, when we made a more extended stop by the seashore at Port Sea, our own gentlemen tried their hand at impromptu cooking; and we ladies were invited to a "home-style" meal prepared by Peter and Werner, with Alvaro as waiter and Johannes tending the fire. It was a gala spread of monster hamburgers and Austrian sausage—with, as a final touch, our favorite dessert of hot Schmarrn, raisin pancakes to be generously covered with applesauce and sugar. Only one of our little group remained quietly unenthusiastic—Father Wasner, whose whole approach to the Schmarrn indicated a manful blending of fortitude and restraint. All unknowing—as we discovered later—he had helped himself to salt instead of sugar.

Between Tamworth and Mudgee, we spent a night on a sheep station—on several sheep stations, since we were distributed for the night among various ranches some miles apart. All kinds of private cars were pressed into service to fetch and carry us, rolling over bumpy dirt roads, or charging axle-deep through brooks and bridgeless streams. Maria and I, as guests of the Kearneys in the "central house," listened at night to the noisy thumping of the kangaroos in the bush and reflected to each other that fourteen thousand acres make a big front yard.

Johannes and Alvaro were having even more excitement. They had been invited to join a kangaroo hunt, going quietly out into the bush in the hush of early evening just before dark. Suddenly, as Alvaro told us later, the silent thickets came alive with startled kangaroos—kangaroos everywhere, leaping and fleeing from the bush to the open spaces, then galloping, galloping, galloping, in a long line of retreating shadows silhouetted against the rosy horizon and the gold of the setting sun. . . .

Little by little, we came to know and appreciate the sturdy individualism of Australian character. We met the great and good shepherds of the Australian flock: in Sydney, Cardinal-Archbishop Gilroy; in Brisbane, Archbishop Duhig; in Melbourne, Archbishop Mannix. Of all of them, Archbishop Mannix remains, perhaps, the most vivid memory. In bearing and appearance, he looked as frail and other-worldly as a carved saint in a Spanish cathedral. Actually, he was over ninety, conducted all diocesan affairs himself and—refusing a car—traveled nearly everywhere on foot. His unannounced appearance in a concert hall could bring an entire audience of twenty-five hundred to its feet. . . .

Was it after such a "surprise appearance" that we sang an encore especially for him? I cannot remember the exact circumstances, but I do remember the song: it was *The Last Rose of Summer*, and the Archbishop was equal to the occasion.

"Thank you very much indeed," he said graciously, as we finished. "I may be 'faded,' but I am not 'gone.'"

With all the other vibrant personalities we came to know and love, I must mention the whole anonymous host of generous friends who, separately or together, taught us to "speak Australian." In my first lesson I mastered two typically Australian expressions: "bonzer" and "my word!"

"If you ask me whether I like you," I wrote home to those in Stowe, "and I say 'My word!'—then you know I really do. And I do: you are all simply 'bonzer'!"

After that it was not so easy. I learned that the new "fridge" can be a "beaut," and that you put the "vedge" in the "fridge." But one or two questions will remain forever unsettled in my mind. Why, for instance, should a man with red hair be called a "blue"? And what, oh what, is a "wooloomooloo yank" or a "willy willy in the never never"? Today, some years later, I find I cannot remember why a "grafter" is better than a "wowser"; and when it comes to distinguishing between a "cocky," a "stockman," and a "bushman," I must say I "drop the bundle." My word!

Not that everyone we met was Australian. Counting up before we left, we realized that we had encountered French, Germans, Americans, Italians, Chinese and Lebanese—plus Father Wasner's nephew; our own Uncle Hans Dreiheller; an Austrian soccer team; Lotte Lehmann's former hairdresser from Vienna; and the Bishop of Fiji. We emerged from each polyglot situation feeling in some way half-American, half-Irish. After all, Foster Browne in New Zealand had written of our singing as "the real McKay." And years before, Father Saunders had called us his "O'Trapps". . . .

An extreme example of international variety was the backstage party we had one night after a concert in Melbourne. We were not really backstage at all, but in the offices of the management upstairs—with an unusual mixture of backgrounds and personalities brought together in one spot. We had invited the Weir brothers, Harry, Herbert, and Sylvester, three superb German comedians appearing in Melbourne at the time, and, with them, a Parisian juggler who could balance himself, on one hand, upon two champagne bottles upturned, neck to neck. There was also an Australian magician—who had been an architect until his eyes failed, and now made more money than if they hadn't. There was Miss Stewart from the management; a French nun who had come with us to the concert; and the Trapp Family Singers—all of us—including, as we did, such disparate names as Pietro LaManna, Alvaro Villa, and Barbara Stechow.

There can be no duplication, in either hemisphere, of that memorable "down under" party. While Werner, Alvaro and

Johannes circulated Austrian Würstl as refreshments, the magician went into his act. A single noodle became longer, and longer, and longer, before our eyes; then one lighted candle became five lighted candles, and went surprisingly back to being one again. Meanwhile, off in one corner, the juggler and the nun discussed mission work, in French; while Annette and Barbara in another taught Harry, Herbert, and Sylvester the poi dance—with such success that the next night the three included it on the stage as part of their act. As Harry and Herbert swung the pois, Sylvester reassured the audience, "Don't worry. This is just a little something we learned from the Trapp Family!" Not even their subsequent appearances with Ed Sullivan's show in New York could equal for me that night in Melbourne when the Weir brothers received our basic instructions.

By way of contrast, we also came to meet the Australian primitives, the Aborigines. In Sydney, Father Wasner, Agathe, and I drove out to visit an aboriginal village, a modest area on the outskirts of the city; and there champion Joe Timbay, a half-caste, threw his boomerang for us. We were fascinated to see the great, wide-angled weapons spin out into the air, describe a long ellipse, and return; and Joe handled them beautifully—first one, then two, then three at a time.

While Joe and his small children were inspecting—dubiously—one of our recorders, an old grandmother of the village was giving me a lengthy explanation of the "deathbone" ritual. The bone, she explained, must be carefully buried so as to point in the direction of the unfortunate person involved. Then chants and incantations are performed above and around the bone, until the desired effect is achieved: the person dies.

"Try it," grandma urged me, while my hair stood on end, "when you really want to be rid of someone."

My heart went out to this superstitious and still primitive people, for whom the world of magic and dreams is as real as their material surroundings, and to whom a "deathbone" is as practical and commonplace as Joe Timbay's boomerang or the munga-wood plates we all bought later in an aboriginal settlement near Melbourne.

The boomerang and the kangaroo are frequently used to symbolize Australia; but, for me, neither of these will do completely. *Waltzing Matilda* must be included, too.

Waltzing Matilda is the Australians' own folk song. Long before we left New Zealand, Father Wasner had worked out a special arrangement and given us a quick vocabulary lesson:

> swagman—tramp
> coolibah—eucalyptus
> billabong—water hole
> matilda—a tramp's bundle

In Wellington, New Zealand, we began to rehearse in earnest:

> "Once a jolly swagman camped by a billabong
> Under the shade of a coolibah tree,
> And he sang as he watched and waited till his billy boiled,
> You'll come a-waltzing, Matilda, with me!"*

Actually the word "waltzing" in this song has nothing to do with dance steps. It means "to go from place to place," or, as we used to say in the old days, *auf die Walz gehen*. Perhaps that is one more reason why the song seemed to me so symbolic. Over and over we sang it as our bus caromed from town to town:

> "And he sang as he watched and waited till his billy boiled,
> You'll come a-waltzing, Matilda, with me!"

The happy-go-lucky air sings of a tramp camped by a riverbank—a tramp who stows a stray sheep into his knapsack, but jumps into the river rather than take rough treatment from the troopers. It is a simple song, but to me its blithe melody represented Australian spirit, Australian determina-

---

* Words by A. B. Paterson, Music by Marie Cowan. Copyright 1936 by Allan & Co., Prop. Ltd. Melbourne, Australia. Copyright 1941 by Carl Fischer, Inc., New York. Reprinted by Permission.

tion, Australian defiance of anything that might be considered oppression. . . .

Up jumped the swagman and sprang into the billabong,
"You'll never catch me alive," said he . . .

Sometimes we were rehearsing, sometimes we were just singing; but with those particular lines our thoughts went backwards in time to the war days when soldier voices carried *Waltzing Matilda* into enemy lines; or to the golden voice of Australia's Marjorie Lawrence, gallantly fighting her way back from polio. . . .

From Sydney on, we took *Waltzing Matilda*, in Father Wasner's new arrangement, to every concert stage.

"Confident reception and enjoyment Australia will be consistent with New Zealand," Mr. Kerridge had wired us in Wellington, and his prediction really held. Our conversations with Mr. Neary in Sydney, however, showed us a first minor difference. In New Zealand we had sung a mere ten concerts a week—how lazy! In Australia we could, and should—and did —average two or more per day. Our itinerary for Sydney, Brisbane, Melbourne and Adelaide read as follows:

10:15 Concert
2:15 Concert
8:15 Concert
Special concert in Y——
Private concert for Z——

In Sydney and Melbourne, morning concerts were planned so that every school child in the city might attend. They came—twenty-five hundred at a time—and made me think of our days at home with the "flower of the nation."

So much in Australia reminded me of the early tours in America. Perhaps it was the small movie houses—the Tivolis, and Rialtos and Strands in which we so often sang. Perhaps it was the vastness of the halls in the larger cities, recalling Lowell, Massachusetts, or the Corn Palace in Mitchell, South Dakota, or any one of the multiple Springfields of our experience. In some indefinite way, I felt at home.

I went on feeling at home—until, suddenly, all at once, I discovered that I was homesick. We were in Melbourne at the time. For months we had been singing our basic repertoire of four programs: sacred music; instrumental groups; madrigals; folk songs. We had come to anticipate the reaction of the audience: a particularly enthusiastic response to the *Tenebrae, Crux Fidelis, Saudade, Turkey in the Straw;* vigorous applause for our encores: *Pokare kare ana,* the poi dance, the *Hawaiian Wedding Song; Waltzing Matilda.* Then, late in October, in Melbourne, we were asked as a special favor to do our own Town Hall Christmas program.

The great "Town Hall" in Melbourne was sold out for the occasion. Somehow, the proper lanterns and candles were located. A tree appeared. We rehearsed. Finally, on that balmy spring evening, I heard myself giving the familiar word of explanation: ". . . then the whole family goes out together through ice and snow to Midnight Mass. . . ." I slipped backstage; and, in the warm, unfamiliar dark of the wings, Father Wasner began the song we knew so well:

"Hirten, auf um Mitternacht . . ."

As the lights went up and his voice reached out into the audience, it was not Aigen-bei-Salzburg and a "whole family going out together through ice and snow" that I saw in my mind's eye, but Town Hall, New York, with the curtains opening; with all the old friends smiling up at us from beyond the footlights—all at once I felt that I was ready to go home.

Today, looking back on Australia, I remember the strange nostalgia of that Christmas concert in Melbourne on a spring evening in October. I can half hear many blithe Australian voices—and our own—singing, "You'll come a-waltzing, Matilda, with me." In my mind's eye I see a long line of kangaroos leaping along the road into the sunset—and far, far behind them comes the little blue bus of the Trapp Family Singers, sturdily, jauntily, leaping too.

24

Of Music and Missions

"If you ever decide to stop singing, let me know," said Archbishop Carboni. As Apostolic Delegate, he had received us when we arrived in Sydney, and several times thereafter. Now, on this November day of our farewell visit, he spoke very solemnly, and we concentrated intently on his words. It is a grave thing to be told that a concert tour has been significant for the history of the Church in New Zealand and Australia. "And I say once again," the Archbishop continued, "that if you ever stop singing, I hope you will think of the great need for music among the far-flung missions of the Faith. I could use every one of you."

Archbishop Carboni is a hearty and vigorous man—fatherly and jolly as well. To talk with him is to feel oneself in the presence of deep human insight, vision, and flexibility—combined with real humility and with the firmness of a heart and will securely grounded in the Heart and Will of Truth. We were so moved by what he said to us that day that one or two of us made notes to be copied down later in full detail.

During our months in Australia we had heard and thought much of the missions—ever since we had first learned of Bishop Arkfeldt, the "Flying Bishop," who visits his New Guinea flock by plane and is his own pilot to bring them the supplies they need.

Then "Ma Mère" and Father Murphy had made us even more mission-conscious. Ma Mère—we never could remember her real name—is a tall, strong Frenchwoman, Superior of a native Order, the Ancillae Domini, at Port Moresby, New Guinea. She had come to Sydney for hospitalization because of a foot injury; then to a concert; then to visit us; then to stay at our hotel; until, finally, we all went on a vacation together. We were all deeply touched by her vibrant personality and sincere dedication, and Maria listened for hours while she explained the work of the Ancillae with native Papuan girls and described in detail their work in nursing the sick and educating little Papuans. I can still see Ma Mère's tall figure in its loose-flowing, belted habit, as she spoke of the importance of human example and the effort of self-discipline required in a situation where one's every gesture will be imitated and where dedication means representing all virtues to the natives. . . .

Father Murphy's mission post is at Rossel Island, to the east of New Guinea. In that remote spot, it seems, he had read *The Story of the Trapp Family Singers*. In that remote spot, too, a hurricane had one day completely destroyed his little mission church. It was just then—in the confusion of all the ruins and destruction—that Father read of our experiences at Cor Unum on that dreadful, blizzardy day in early spring, when the house we were building suddenly fell, chimney, pipes, and all, straight down into the cellar. "If they could build it up again," said Father Murphy to himself, "why can't we?" And, calling the natives to him, he set them all to work.

The new church now stands on Rossel Island—a beautiful, grass-bound, native structure with a wide-angle roof—built to combine loving vision with native skill in construction, and symbolizing on that wind-swept island the power of faith and of hope.

Both Ma Mère and Father Murphy are under the jurisdiction of the Apostolic Delegate and Ma Mère was present at this farewell visit. There were echoes in our ears of important past discussions we had had together, talking of what can happen when a native mind, a "primitive" intelligence, is educated away from the limitations of its tribal customs and taboos. So often, too, we had gone over, and with various possible solutions, the basic problem of how a missionary can hope to make himself understood by people whose language he cannot speak. . . .

This question we had so frequently raised together seemed now to enter directly into what Archbishop Carboni was saying about the need in missions for the universal language of music. "I could use every one of you," he repeated.

At that point an impatient taxi horn blew from outside. It was time to leave. "Your Excellency," I said quickly, "now that we are all together for the last time, will you give us your blessing?"

"Gladly," he answered—and we knelt in silence at his feet.

For some time we had known that once we were home again there would be only a brief pre-Christmas tour. After that the Trapp Family Singers would no longer sing. The decision, for the many reasons already mentioned, had at last been taken. And though nothing was said, Archbishop Carboni's understanding expression, as we turned to go, plainly showed us that he knew it.

Farewell Concert

So, at long last, we came home. A concert in Fiji; a stopover in Honolulu—disappointing because it was too rainy to attempt the flying visit we had hoped to make to the colony at Molokai; then, finally, on November 16, 1955, San Francisco. Annette headed for Ogden, Utah, and Barbara for Oberlin, Ohio—each hoping for a quick reunion with her family before the final weeks of the Christmas tour. At Chicago, Alvaro got out. The rest of us reached La Guardia airport late at night, and with spirits as limp as the last of our wilted carnation leis. Illi and Rosemary Glynn, waving frantically, were a welcome sight.

The last tour seemed to begin almost at once, and to end just as quickly. I remember New Rochelle, New York, on December sixth; Setauket, Long Island; Washington, D. C. It was all real and unreal at the same time, and I could not seem to believe that this was final.

For our last day in Town Hall, the house was full and, as the lights dimmed and the familiar maroon curtains parted, a great wave of loving applause rushed up to us over the footlights. Yes, there were the familiar faces. As a special joyous surprise, in the first row, sat our entire "home-staff" from Cor Unum: Julie, Rosemary and Illi had driven all day to be with us, and would drive all night to return. And, uniting the Vermont present with the Philadelphia past, Sophie Drinker was in the audience.

It seemed fitting to bring back at last to our own home
stage the songs we had traveled so far to find: *Waltzing Matilda*, the poi dance, the *Hawaiian Wedding Song*; but the
preferred songs on the program that day were the old "tradi-
tionals" that our family of Christmas friends had come to
expect: *The Virgin's Lullaby* and *Stille Nacht*. To these we
had added Johannes Brahms' *Abschiedslied—Song of Parting*:

> "The day has come when thou and I
> My dearest one, must say goodbye.
> I leave my heart behind with thee;
> So far away, but it must be.
> Far, far away, far, far away."

We began the second verse:

> "I need no promise, ask no vow,
> And I will be as true as thou—"

All at once, and for no particular reason, I was surrounded
with memories of the past . . . of Lorli and Illi playing their
recorders for the first time on the stage, their pigtails flying
in the excitement of effort; of our ten-foot Christmas tree hung
with cookies. I thought of how four-year-old Johannes had
begged to do *Old MacDonald* as a solo; and then flatly refused to sing when the great moment came. I saw Martina
heading off-stage at the intermission to where a smiling
Canadian boy waited in the wings. I saw Rupert and Werner
suddenly surprising us backstage by arriving on leave during
the war in their uniforms of the United States Army. . . .

> "Each night, each morning, I will pray,
> 'God keep thee safe when I'm away.'
> Far, far away, far, far away."

Behind me, an imaginary apple seemed to drop with a
thud from a remembered tree—and a fat little boy in blue
waddled over to pick it up.

I missed my husband. . . .

When the time came for encores, our hearts overflowed

with wanting to meet every single request, from the *Echo Song* to the old, familiar *Children's Blessing,* learned by all of us ·so long ago in Sweden on that famous day when Lorli and Illi came down with the measles.

> "Oh, Jesus, Lord divine,
> Protect this child of mine. . . ."

We could have sung all night, and no one wanted to go home. Then at last, with absolute finality—because there was another concert scheduled to follow ours—the great maroon curtains came together.

"Now it is really ended," I told myself, not in the least convinced. Later, press reports spoke of "inspired direction" and "lasting, overwhelming, world-wide popularity." It was consoling to know—as we knew in truth—that we had never sung better. I could hear Father Wasner voicing the feeling of all of us to those who crowded backstage:

"But we hope it does not end. We hope that what we have done will carry—out into the families who have heard us and, from them, to others. . . ."

At that moment nothing could have been farther from my mind than plans for the future and the words of Archbishop Carboni in Sydney. I just knew that I could not believe we had completed our farewell tour. It was not until that Christmas morning, in the cold dawn of my room at Stowe, as I stood at the window seeing the ship's lantern burning steadily, that I began once again to remember what my husband had not wanted us to forget: in the adventure of faith there is no such thing as a last encore. "The end" means a new beginning. "Whenever God closes a door, He opens a window."

A *Chapter After the Last*

Archbishop Carboni did not forget us. Spring and summer came to Cor Unum; then, in November, Maria, Rosmarie and Johannes left at his invitation to spend a year with the missions in New Guinea. One month later, also at the Archbishop's suggestion, Monsignor Wasner and I departed for a tour of the South Sea islands—an exhaustive tour that was to take us around the globe and keep us many months from home.

In the course of our travels, we came to know torrid wet heat, and swamps, and insects. We encountered tropical infections and malaria. We were taken in small boats over incredibly rough stretches of water, while Father Wasner and I, literally, stood on our heads to avoid being tossed into the choppy seas. We followed jungle roads and crossed, on makeshift logs, over swift muddy streams infested with crocodiles. We flew for a week with Bishop Arkfeldt.

One of our visits was to the high-valley areas of New Guinea only recently discovered by the white man. There, truly on the edge of civilization, we entered smoky, smelly huts where husband, wives(?), children, pigs and potatoes were all piled together in the darkness. We encountered also the spiritual darkness of sorcery and witchcraft surrounding their lives, as we saw that each house had its own "head-shrine"—a post with the skull of a parent or child fastened to it.

We saw the heroic work of the missions. . . . I shall never forget a certain Benediction on a small South Sea island surrounded by coral reefs and blue sea, where all the old native warriors followed the priest in procession. They still carried their war clubs and axes. They still carried their ancient spears, but with the heads pointing downwards as a sign of peace. During Benediction they raised these old weapons high in the air before the altar of the Prince of Peace, while outside the blue sea glittered and the white breakers crashed against the reef.

We had been traveling nearly a year before we came to Budoya and to our own three from Cor Unum. We found Maria making sick calls by bicycle to the neighboring villages, and running a coop-like "hospital" built by Johannes. All three were teaching school and catechism classes; and as I knelt on the rough gravel of the church floor, I could hear Rosmarie's voice giving an English lesson in the straw-thatched, windowless school close by:

"Today, I go; yesterday, I *went* . . ."

On our first day there, after lunch, I lay down on my bed for a rest, half listening to the voices of a little group of native boys cutting and raking grass outside. They were singing. . . . Suddenly, I realized that the tune was our own familiar pilgrimage hymn, *Meerstern ich dich grüsse*, but they had substituted their own words: *Kamatoi oyo*. As I listened, they changed to O *maimiyo Jesu*, O *Haupt voll Blut und Wuden*—which Maria told me later is a great favorite. If Johann Sebastian Bach could have known that his chorale from the *Saint Matthew Passion* would be sung with such fervor by the grandchildren of some of the most ferocious cannibals of the South Seas!

Father Wasner says that, musically, many of these natives are still in the Stone Age and that some tribes have only five tones, or even fewer. At first, they seem to have no feeling for our intervals or scales, yet with even a little instruction they can become capable of incredible precision and purity of tone. . . . One day, when I overheard the little grass-cutters singing *Good Night to You All* and *Viva la Musica*, I had the weird feeling that our Music Camp was again in

session. It was August, and just about time for the third Sing
Week. . . .

Rosmarie, Maria and Johannes stayed much longer in New
Guinea than they had originally planned. As I write today,
they are still in Budoya, though they expect soon to leave
for home. Monsignor Wasner and I, after many months away,
are also about to return—from Rome where there have been
important talks with the Society for the Propagation of the
Faith. Our long absence has meant that Ruth Murdoch, a
dear friend of Cor Unum and of mine, took over for me the
final editing of A *Family on Wheels*; and to Rosemary Glynn
went the heroic task of typing an entire manuscript with the
author halfway round the world.

In a few months, God willing, we shall all be together
again. Already, Hedwig is scanning Luce Hill for the proper
Christmas tree—and this year, along with *Stille Nacht* and
Hirten auf, there will be two new songs: *Kamatoi oyo* and
O maimiyo Jesu. . . .

So once again our wheels come rolling home. *The Story of
the Trapp Family Singers* began with a "Chapter Before the
First" and A *Family on Wheels* ends with a "Chapter After
the Last." Music-minded and mission-minded, Cor Unum
looks to the future. Who knows—perhaps this Chapter After
the Last is really the beginning of another book?

Innsbruck
Austria
1958